SpringerBriefs in Law

SpringerBriefs present concise summaries of cutting-edge research and practical applications across a wide spectrum of fields. Featuring compact volumes of 50 to 125 pages, the series covers a range of content from professional to academic. Typical topics might include:

- A timely report of state-of-the art analytical techniques
- A bridge between new research results, as published in journal articles, and a contextual literature review
- A snapshot of a hot or emerging topic
- A presentation of core concepts that students must understand in order to make independent contributions

SpringerBriefs in Law showcase emerging theory, empirical research, and practical application in Law from a global author community. SpringerBriefs are characterized by fast, global electronic dissemination, standard publishing contracts, standardized manuscript preparation and formatting guidelines, and expedited production schedules.

Catherine S. Namakula
Editor

Untold Reflections from the World Conference Against Racism

From Durban to Humanity

Springer

Editor
Catherine S. Namakula
Africa Reparation Hub, Faculty of Law
University of the Free State
Bloemfontein, South Africa

ISSN 2192-855X ISSN 2192-8568 (electronic)
SpringerBriefs in Law
ISBN 978-3-032-17264-8 ISBN 978-3-032-17265-5 (eBook)
https://doi.org/10.1007/978-3-032-17265-5

This Springer imprint is published by the registered company Springer Nature Switzerland AG
The registered company address is: Gewerbestrasse 11, 6330 Cham, Switzerland

To the current and future generations, this book chronicles and analyses how humanity successfully agreed to eliminate racism and other forms of intolerance. The truth about Durban is revealed.

Hon. Litha Musyimi – Ogana, Commissioner, African Commission on Human and Peoples' Rights.

This excellent book is a timely account of the historic 2001 UN World Conference Against Racism, whose 'Programme and Plan of Action represents one of the greatest, but little known, victories of African people in the international arena'. It is quite appropriate that it is coming out during this centenary of Pan-African icons Malcolm X, Frantz Fanon, and Patrice Lumumba.

Roger Wareham, International human rights attorney and founding member of the December 12th Movement International Secretariat.

What a pity that the World Conference against Racism in Durban is only remembered for the fierce controversies over whether Zionism should be condemned as a form of racism. This book reminds us that there were many other issues, where African experience, imagination, and advocacy played a special role, on which groundbreaking consensus was reached.

Albie Sachs, Former Justice of the Constitutional Court of South Africa

Foreword

The 2001 World Conference against Racism, Racial Discrimination, Xenophobia and Related Intolerance, which took place in Durban, South Africa, was undoubtedly a global historic event. It attracted almost 19,000 participants from all over the world, including delegates from approximately 170 UN Member States, representatives of non-governmental organizations, UN agencies, national human rights institutions, and international and local media. The Conference was also a symbolic event. The then UN Secretary-General Kofi Annan stressed in his opening address to the Conference that: '[e]veryone of us must feel the symbolism of this moment—the conjunction of theme [United against racism], time and place'. He rightly added: '[w]here else, my friends, could we hold this conference? Who else could teach us how to overcome racism, discrimination and intolerance, if not the people of this country?'

Indeed, South Africa demonstrated its leading role throughout the preparatory process, and, in particular, at pivotal moments of the Conference. Many other States and actors played an important role during the intense negotiations of the final documents—the Durban Declaration and Programme of Action (DDPA). The authors of this book highlight the contributions of numerous actors. In addition, the role of the Group of 21, comprising four States from each of the five UN regional groups, and chaired by South Africa, in restructuring and streamlining the draft documents for final negotiations, deserves mentioning.

When you read experts' analyses, articles, and the press from various corners of the world about the preparatory process, the report of Conference proceedings itself, and the post-Durban 2001 developments, you will often find diametrically opposed assessments and interpretations of events, as well as the Conference's final documents. The views range from welcoming and positive to openly hateful and denouncing. Therefore, this book, which contains a first-hand factual account written by renowned experts who participated in the Conference in different capacities and contributed to its successful outcome, is of particular value. The book lifts the curtain on the little-known moments of how negotiating positions of States and regional groups were brought to a consensus outcome, and how solutions to the most controversial and seemingly insurmountable stalemates were found.

The authors reveal the dramatic atmosphere at the Conference and the complexity of the negotiations, emotionally connecting and engaging the reader with the event. The book sheds light on the notion of the 'victims of racism' and 'racial discrimination', as defined by the Durban Declaration. It illuminates the breakthrough agreement on the issues of 'the past' and the causal nexus of crimes of slavery and slave trade, and other harmful practices, with the current situation of Africans, people of African descent, people of Asian descent, and indigenous peoples. It may also help to dispel myths, misperceptions, and disinformation about the Conference, its follow-up process, and related meetings, in particular, concerning the Durban Declaration and Programme of Action consensus paragraphs relating to the situation in the Middle East at the time and the right to security for all States in the region, including Israel, and the plight of the Palestinian people under foreign occupation.

Addressing the Conference on 1 September 2001 in a video message, the first democratically elected President of South Africa, Nelson Mandela, said that racism is often described as a disease that affects the mind and the soul, and that it is a problem for all of us. 'The tragedy is', he continued, 'that a cure is within our reach, yet we have not seized it. To conquer racism, we must administer a treatment that is comprehensive and holistic'. It is highly regrettable that more than 25 years after the adoption of the Durban Declaration and Programme of Action, which provided a holistic vision and equipped the international community with the necessary tools to effectively tackle and eradicate racism and racial discrimination, the world is still divided and unable to honour this common commitment.

Moscow, Russia Yury Boychenko

Preface

This book is intended to demystify the substantive and procedural undertakings of the World Conference against Racism, Racial Discrimination, Xenophobia and Related Intolerance of 2001, leading up to the proclamation of the Durban Declaration and Programme of Action (DDPA), the most comprehensive and visionary human rights framework against the thorny subjects. The Conference was held in Durban, South Africa (31 August–07 September 2001) preceded by regional preparatory conferences in Strasbourg (11–13 October 2000), Santiago de Chile (5–7 December 2000), Dakar (22–24 January 2001), and Teheran (19–21 February 2001).

This book contains seven revealing contributions from international luminaries that propelled the Durban process including Dr. Bertrand Ramcharan (Guyana), the UN Deputy High Commissioner for Human Rights during the time of the Durban Conference, and drafter of the draft declaration and programme of action for the [unsuccessful] 1978, the 1983 conference, and the draft that was tabled before the preparatory committee of the Conference of 2001; Prof. Marc Bossuyt (Belgium), Chairperson/Rapporteur of the Working Group on the draft declaration; Gay McDougall (USA), participant in the Durban Conference and its preparatory committees and Vice Chairperson of the UN Committee on the Elimination of Racial Discrimination (CERD); H.E Ambassador Silvio José Albuquerque e Silva (Brazil), member of the Brazilian delegation to the Durban Conference, and Pastor Murillo (Colombia), alternate head of the delegation of Colombia to the Santiago regional preparatory conference (of the Americas), and the Durban Conference. Accounts of delegates of South Africa to the Durban Conference, Ambassador Abdul Samad Minty, and Advocate Gumbi Mojankunyane, are included.

The publication of this book is part of the pioneering high-level campaign I initiated as Chairperson of the Working Group of experts on people of African descent. Following the boycott of the UN General Assembly commemoration of 20 years of the Durban Conference and the DDPA by an increasing number of member states in September 2021, I realized that disseminating knowledge and fostering uncensored dialogue about the making of the DDPA would justify the legitimacy of the noble framework from the disinformation and misinformation that was gaining leverage following the transition of the persons that propelled the Durban process. The

Working Group supported my proposal of holding a special state-led session on *Memoirs of Durban by the Legends of Durban* during the 32nd public session of the special procedure of the Human Rights Council in Geneva in 2022. The Chair of the special event, Ambassador Mxolisi Nkosi, the Permanent Representative of South Africa to the United Nations Office at Geneva noted that 'while the Durban Declaration and Programme of Action remained a significant achievement in the global struggle against racism and racial discrimination, more work needed to be done to achieve its goals, and it's the responsibility of all stakeholders to work together to make sure that its cause was realized'.[1] Ambassador Abdul Minty decried the unfounded nature of claims that the DDPA is anti-Semitic and racist (in reverse).

In the first chapter, Dr. Ramcharan delineates *the struggle for racial justice at the Durban Conference* in the track record of the UN since the proclamation of the UN Charter, to the first, second, and third World Conferences against Racism. He describes the intense political environment that characterized the Conference and the sensitive political issues that were on the agenda while recognizing specific luminaries for their diplomacy and tact in negotiating the sharp edges. Dr. Ramcharan clarifies the vision of the nations, and the UN, to implement the Durban Declaration and Programme of Action.

In an exposition of Procedural Issues at the World Conference against Racism in the second chapter, Prof. Bossuyt explains the way the controversial paragraphs were handled in the final hours of the Durban Conference, a dramatic procedural battle characterized by four suspensions of the meetings of the Main Committee and a special appeal for an outcome by the President to the Conference. He details the labours of Durban structures in preserving consensus amidst immense pressure for a vote.

In the third chapter, Prof. Bossuyt clarifies the origins of the Durban Conference and the evolution of the structures that supported the preparations and the deliberations of the Conference. He boldly engages with the unbalanced criticism levelled against it, without regard for the adverse circumstances that prevailed such as the inherently delicate nature of the themes addressed, the radical inflexibility of Western governments, their frequent disruption of deliberations, and the scepticism from even some of the first appointed chairpersons of the Working Group on the draft declaration about the prospects of success of the task they were entrusted with. Prof. Bossuyt reveals the 'leadership code' and approach he utilized to successfully steer Working Group I through the negotiations about negotiations, and the negotiations of the declaration and programme of action.

The fourth chapter analyses the narratives of Ambassador Minty and Advocate Gumbi in an elucidation of the controversy that ensued at the NGO forum preceding the Conference, which nearly affected its credibility. The chapter details the Durban structures for dialogue and the workflow in the framework of the negotiations that were characterized by extensive compromises. It examines the philosophies

[1] See Report of the Working Group of experts on people of African descent, A/HRC/54/67, 21 July 2023, para 80.

advanced in support of the predetermined rigid US position, and its obstructionist tactics that subsist today.

Whereas each author inevitably alludes to the legacy of the World Conference against Racism from a unique perspective, Prof. McDougall's analysis titled '*A Retrospective of the 2001 World Conference against Racism*' (in the fifth chapter) addresses the achievements of Durban in concrete terms while tackling the criticisms of the Durban outcomes simultaneously. Prof. McDougall convincingly engages with the origins of the claims of anti-Semitism at the Durban Conference.

The sixth chapter reveals Brazil's commitment and its contribution to the Durban process from the regional conference in Santiago. Brazil is home to the largest black population outside Africa. Ambassador Silva explains the distinctiveness and alienation of the fight against racism and racial discrimination among states, and the resolve of the Brazilian delegation to be firm and determined to maximize the favourable context of Durban and positively influence the difficult negotiations. He explains the tact of Brazil in submitting a motion for non-consideration of Syria's proposal for the Main Committee to reconsider three of the most controversial paragraphs of the draft of the Durban Declaration and Programme of Action on the last day of the Conference. Ambassador Silva explains why Brazil eventually withdrew its no action motion.

In the seventh chapter,[2] Pastor Elias Martínez Murillo examines the unprecedented recognition accorded, by the Durban process and its outcomes, to people of African descent as subjects of international law while centring the key role of the Santiago conference. He contributes perspectives of the region with the greatest number of persons of African descent, with advanced discourse on the legacies of the past. He traces the opposition to the Durban Conference and its outcomes to coercive diplomatic actions by the United States of America prior to the Conference, encouraging states to withdraw. He regrets the lost decade of setbacks in human rights, which followed the attacks of September 11, 2001, three days after the Durban Conference. He explains the continuity of the Durban process through its post-conference mechanisms such as the UN Working Group of experts on people of African descent, the nexus between Durban and the International Decade on people of African descent, and the prospects of an International Declaration on the Respect, Protection and Realization of the Human Rights of People of African Descent.

My successor, Dr. Barbara Reynolds (Abena) concludes this book with a prospective view on *Making the Most of the Legendary Leadership and Legacy of Durban*. She interrogates the legacy of the Durban conference as majorly stimulating attention to concerns of people of African descent, with minimal successful action to transform the lived experiences of the people. Racism subsists. She urges stakeholders to prioritize racial justice, reparatory justice, environmental and spatial justice, and digital justice.

---

[2] The Spanish version in the annex is the authoritative version.

The Legends of Durban regard their contribution(s) to this book as critical in clarifying to humanity the importance of the highest level accorded to all the substantive matters addressed comprehensively by the Conference, and the integrity of the process at Durban. This book is the one truth about the inner workings of the World Conference against Racism from the leaders themselves. They confirm the success and achievements of the Durban Conference encapsulated in the Durban Declaration and Programme of Action. The authors express mutually reinforcing content in certain respects, as confirmation and reinforcement of the truth about the Durban process and outcomes. Following the spirit of Durban and the resilience that characterized its formulation, the DDPA is inherently indomitable. Even those that supposedly reject it seem subconsciously guided by its principles, a confirmation of its stance as the most comprehensive, instructive, and action-oriented international framework for fighting discrimination and intolerance. The DDPA offers a road map for racial justice that reinforces the foundations laid by the ICERD (International Convention on the Elimination of All Forms of Racial Discrimination) regime for 60 years, and it continues to resiliently navigate politically motivated contention that began before it existed. The role of human rights mechanisms and civil society in furthering the Durban process and supporting humanity not to walk back from its own noble commitment is noteworthy.

Bloemfontein, South Africa Catherine S. Namakula

Contents

The Struggle for Racial Justice at the Durban Conference

Bertrand Ramcharan

1 Introduction

The Durban World Conference against racism, racial discrimination, xenophobia and related forms of intolerance, held in 2001, laid down strategies to promote racial equality and justice world-wide that have been pursued for the past quarter of a century, and that will continue to provide the foundations for future activities in this area in the coming decades. This chapter offers glimpses into the substantive organization of the conference, traces its principal outcomes, and discusses some of the substantive and political issues that had to be overcome to achieve agreement at Durban.

The Durban Conference has to be viewed in the intellectual, policy and political streams of the efforts of the United Nations since its establishment to work for equality and non-discrimination. Before the Durban Conference, there had probably never been as difficult a conference like it in the history of the United Nations. There were a number of currents running in the approach to, and at, the Conference. First, there was the quest of Africans and the African diaspora for recognition of the historical injustices of slavery. Second, there were claims for justice from communities in different parts of the world. And third, there was the situation then prevailing in the Middle East.

Dr. Bertrand Ramcharan, Deputy UN High Commissioner for Human Rights (during the Durban Conference).
Seventh Chancellor of the University of Guyana. Previously: Deputy and then Acting UN High Commissioner for Human Rights; Professor at the Geneva Graduate Institute of International and Development Studies; Commissioner of the International Commission of Jurists.

B. Ramcharan (✉)
Geneva, Switzerland

C. S. Namakula (ed.), *Untold Reflections from the World Conference Against Racism*, SpringerBriefs in Law, https://doi.org/10.1007/978-3-032-17265-5_1

At the start of the twenty-first century, communities across the globe were making strong claims for justice, including for inter-generational justice. From a human rights perspective, one had to acknowledge those claims for justice while negotiating the political pitfalls involved. One should also bear in mind that the Conference took on strong emotional significance for participants stemming from the fact that it was taking place in South Africa, the land of Nelson Mandela, the land of the historic struggle against apartheid. That added something unique, something that could be sensed in and around the halls of the Conference.

It was of great value to have the Conference in South Africa. The South African authorities gave of their utmost by way of hospitality and services. The hospitality and facilities came from the heart and were received as such. For a start, it is necessary to set the Durban Conference in the perspective of the historic efforts of the United Nations to promote racial equality and justice, including through the two preceding world conferences on racism and racial discrimination in 1978 and 1983 respectively.

1.1 Intellectual and Policy Antecedents

The United Nations Charter underscored the commitment of the Peoples of the United Nations to work for universal respect for human rights without discrimination on grounds of race, sex, language or religion. The Universal Declaration of Human Rights advanced this commitment and added its historic statement that all human beings are born free and equal in dignity and respect. They are endowed with reason and conscience and should act towards one another in a spirit of brotherhood – and sisterhood!

The UN Special Committee on Decolonization and the UN Special Committee against Apartheid made pioneering contributions to the struggle for self-determination and equality. The adoption of the International Convention on the Elimination of all Forms of Racial Discrimination in 1965 brought in reporting and petitions' procedures to concretize the quest for equality world-wide.

The pioneering study on Racial Discrimination, written by Jose Santa Cruz of Chile for the UN Sub-Commission on Prevention of Discrimination and Protection of Minorities broke new ground in this area and remains to this day an indispensable reference work on strategies to combat racial discrimination.[1]

The proclamation of an International Day against Racial Discrimination, an International Year against Racial Discrimination, and successive decades for action to combat racism and racial discrimination attested to the determination of the United Nations to stamp out racism and racial discrimination.

[1] See, Santa Cruz, Hernán, Racial Discrimination Study: Revised and Updated Version, Special Rapporteur of the Sub-Commission on Prevention of Discrimination and Protection of Minorities, 1976. UN publication, Sales No.E.76.XIV.2. https://searchlibrary.ohchr.org/record/18167?ln=en: Accessed 13 June 2025.

The holding of three world conferences against racism and racial discrimination, in 1978, 1983, and 2001 was meant to rally the world behind the cause of racial equality. This author was a member of the UN human rights secretariat in all three world conferences and prepared the draft declarations and programmes of action for all three of them. The draft declaration and programme of action we prepared for the 1978 conference was never acted upon because the conference broke down due to political disagreements amongst states. The Secretary-General of the Conference, Mr C.V. Narasimhan, withheld the draft until it was too late for the delegates to consider and to take action on it.

In the aftermath of the 1978 conference, the Secretariat unit assigned to the Decade for Action to Combat Racism and Racial Discrimination, led by Dr Emmanuel Mompoint (Haiti), my friend, and with the support of this author, who was then Special Assistant to the Director of the Division of Human Rights decided to act on four fronts between 1978 and 1983: first to study and organize seminars on recourse procedures for victims of racism and racial discrimination in different regions of the world;[2] second, to study the role of community relations commissions; third, to study the role of professors and directors of race relations institutions on the teaching of problems of racial discrimination;[3] fourth to develop model legislation for the implementation of the International Convention on the Elimination of Racial Discrimination.[4] All four areas were implemented, with significant reports emanating from them.

At the second world conference, in 1983, James O.C. Jonah the Secretary-General of the conference, asked for, and this author prepared a draft declaration and programme of action, which was placed before the drafting committee of the conference. The second world conference came up with a notable declaration and programme of action, highlighting the urgency of acting against racism and racial discrimination, and also calling for attention to violations of human rights against persons belonging to minorities, migrants, and to indigenous populations.[5]

By the time the third world conference (the Durban Conference) approached, this author was Deputy High Commissioner for Human Rights, and the then High

---

[2] See for example, Report of the Seminar on Recourse Procedures Available to Victims of Racism and Racial Discrimination and Activities Undertaken at the Regional Level, Geneva 9-20 July 1979. UN doc. ST/HR/SER.A/3, United Nations. New York, 1979.

[3] See, Round Table of University Professors and Directors of Race Relations Institutions on the Teaching of Problems of Racial Discrimination, Geneva, 5-9 November 1979. UN doc. ST/HR/SER.A/5, United Nations, Geneva, 1979. https://digitallibrary.un.org/record/13974?ln=en. Accessed 13 June 2025.

[4] See also, Committee on the Elimination of Racial Discrimination and the Progress Made Towards the Achievement of the Objectives of the International Convention on the Elimination of All Forms of Racial Discrimination. Published on the occasion of the World Conference to Combat Racism and Racial Discrimination, Geneva, 14-25 August 1978. United Nations publication, Sales No. E.79.XIV.4, New York, 1970.

[5] See, UN doc. E/CN.4/1999/WG.1/BP.1 of 9 March 1999: The Declarations and Programmes of Action Adopted by the First (1978) and the Second (1993) World Conferences to Combat Racism and Racial Discrimination.

Commissioner, Ms. Mary Robinson proposed to him to be the Secretary-General of the Conference. However, this author thought that the Conference could benefit from the stature of the High Commissioner as former President of Ireland. Mary Robinson accepted this and became Secretary-General of the Conference. This author worked closely with her and prepared the first drafts of the proposed declaration and programme of action of the Conference.

The secretariat's draft declaration and programme of action was placed before an inter-governmental drafting committee, which took charge and highlighted issues such as the claim for compensation for slavery, the situation of the Palestinians, the situation of the Dalits in India, and the issue of the treatment of persons of African descent. The draft declaration and programme of action that went before the Durban Conference thus bore the imprint of governments, and there would be big political issues to thrash out at Durban. India would not accept discussion of the situation of the Dalits. Arab countries wanted Israel to be criticized for its treatment of Palestinians in the occupied Arab territories, and Western governments led by the United States of America (USA) would not allow this. Caribbean countries insisted on compensation for slavery, and Afro-Caribbean countries insisted on special attention henceforth to persons of African descent. Surrounding the Durban Conference were allegations by Jewish groups of anti-Semitism before and during the Conference. These charges have not gone away.

That the Durban Conference did adopt a declaration and programme of action was quite an achievement for which the President of the Conference, the then South African Minister of Foreign Affairs, Dr. Nkosazana Dlamini Zuma and the Secretary-General of the Conference, Mary Robinson deserve the appreciation of the international community. The Durban Declaration and Programme of Action (DDPA) has several highlights and notable innovations.

2 Highlights of the Durban Declaration and Programme of Action

The Durban Declaration described victims of racism, racial discrimination, xenophobia, and related intolerance as individuals or groups of individuals who are or have been negatively affected by, subjected to, or targets of those scourges.[6] It recognized that people of African descent had been victims of racism, discrimination, and enslavement and of history's denial of their rights for centuries.[7] It also recognized that they, as well as Asians and people of Asian descent, faced barriers as a result of social biases and discrimination.[8]

---

[6] Durban Declaration and Programme of Action, 2001, para 1.

[7] Ibid para 34.

[8] Ibid paras 35, 36.

Strongly condemning racism and discrimination against migrants and the stereotypes often applied to them, the declaration reaffirmed the responsibility of states to protect their human rights and the responsibility of governments to safeguard and protect them against illegal or violent acts perpetrated with racist or xenophobic motivation.[9]

Noting that racism, discrimination, and xenophobia contributed to forced displacement and movement of people as refugees and asylum seekers, the declaration recognized that intolerance against refugees, asylum seekers, and internally displaced persons continued despite efforts to combat them. It underlined the urgency of addressing the root causes of displacement and of finding durable solutions, particularly voluntary return to countries of origin and resettlement in third countries.[10]

The Declaration recognized the existence of intolerance against religious communities, particularly limitations on their right to practice their beliefs freely, as well as the emergence of increased negative stereotyping, hostile acts, and violence against such communities because of their religious beliefs and their ethnic or so-called racial origins.[11]

The Declaration strongly reaffirmed that victims of human rights violations resulting from racism, discrimination, xenophobia and intolerance should be assured access to justice. Access to justice included legal assistance where appropriate, and effective and appropriate protection and remedies, including the right to seek just and adequate reparation or satisfaction for any damage suffered.[12]

The Declaration condemned the persistence and resurgence of neo-nazism, neo-fascism, and violent nationalist ideologies based on racial or national prejudice.[13] It also condemned political platforms and organizations based on racism, xenophobia, or doctrines of racial superiority and related discrimination; and legislation and practices based on racism, discrimination, xenophobia and intolerance as incompatible with democracy and with transparent and accountable governance.[14]

2.1 *Innovations at the Durban Conference*

One may highlight the following innovations at the Durban Conference:

(a) The Conference began tackling the issue that there is only one human race and therefore norms and policies must reflect this reality.
(b) The Conference emphasized that one must build on the basis of human and cultural diversity.

---

[9] Ibid para 48.
[10] Ibid para 54.
[11] Ibid para 60.
[12] Ibid para 104.
[13] Ibid para 84.
[14] Ibid para 84.

(c) The Conference furthered the victims-oriented approach to discrimination. It gave a voice to many victims.
(d) The Conference began the process of broadening the grounds of discrimination and also recognized that multiple and intersectoral forms of discrimination must be dealt with.
(e) In its recognition that slavery and the slave trade were unconscionable, the Conference began the process of tackling inter-generational claims for justice.
(f) The Conference tackled discrimination in respect of economic, social and cultural rights, as well as civil and political rights. The role of positive action was emphasized.
(g) The Conference began the process of generating international attention to the role of the internet in spreading and combating discrimination.[15]
(h) In addition to the problems of minorities, migrants, and indigenous peoples dealt with at previous world conferences, the Durban Conference highlighted, for the first time, the problems of persons of African descent, Romas and the victims of trafficking.
(i) The issue of racial profiling received international attention for the first time.[16]
(j) The impact of poverty and globalization on discrimination was highlighted at the Conference. The role of international financial institutions in combating discrimination was also given attention.[17]
(k) The role of the media and of communications channels was emphasized.[18]
(l) Novel follow-up arrangements were decided upon at Durban.[19]

3 The Political Environment Around the Durban Conference

The foregoing achievements were made notwithstanding intensive political difficulties. At the outset of the Conference, although the USA had someone physically present in Durban, they announced that they were disassociating themselves from the Conference because of alleged acts of anti-Semitism and because the USA would not countenance the idea of reparations for slavery. For a time, there was confusion about whether the USA was participating or not. In the end, it did not.

Outside the conference room, Jewish groups felt that there had been incidents of anti-Semitism and there was a tense atmosphere among the NGOs representatives. We cannot speak to this issue because we were locked in the inter-governmental deliberations. Countries such as Canada also let it be known that they were ready to quit the Conference if anything was about to be considered or adopted that would be

[15] Ibid para 90.
[16] Ibid para 72.
[17] Ibid para 152.
[18] Ibid para 88.
[19] Ibid paras 107–122.

prejudicial to the interests of Israel. This author had sensitive conversations with the Canadian representative, whom he knew well, and with whom he had good personal and professional relations. It took some effort to keep the Canadian delegation in the Conference. There were other delegations that were in a similar situation as Canada.

A positive and constructive role in bringing about consensus was played by the Belgian Foreign Minister, Mr. Louis Michel who sought to provide a political bridge between the Western group of nations and other groups calling for reparations for slavery and for direct criticism of Israel's treatment of the Palestinians. He helped achieve a positive outcome at the Conference.

The President of the Conference, the South African Foreign Minister, Dr Zuma, and the Secretary-General of the Conference, Mrs. Robinson, worked tirelessly and imaginatively to help produce a positive outcome. One of the notable initiatives of Mrs. Robinson was to persuade countries to sign vision statements on policies for racial justice in the future.

3.1 Sensitive Political Issues to Be Negotiated

Two issues that could have broken the Conference were the issue of compensation for slavery; and the issue of Israel's treatment of the Palestinians. The Brazilian representative at the Conference, Ambassador Saboia, played a very constructive role in steering the negotiations towards agreed language on the issue of compensation for slavery.

The drafting groups of the Conference did not address the second issue as the President of the Conference let it be known that, in view of the sensitivities involved, she would be putting forward some proposals as President. Up to the penultimate day of the Conference, we had not yet seen any proposals of the President, who let it be known that she would announce her proposals on the final day.

On the penultimate day, the *Chef-de-Cabinet* of the Secretary-General called this writer to inquire how the Conference was developing. This author informed him that the outcome of the Conference would depend on the proposals on Palestine to be tabled by the President, but that we had no idea what was forth-coming. The *Chef-de-Cabinet* advised the UN Secretary-General, Kofi Annan, who was then vacationing in Scandinavia. Kofi Annan called the President of the Conference and suggested that she show us the proposals she intended to table. She agreed, and so advised Mary Robinson.

Mary Robinson asked that this author be available to consult with the President on her proposals. I was on call to see the President's draft from 4.00 pm on the penultimate day and waited until called in to see her at 4.00 am the following day. When the President showed me her proposals, which I have among my papers, in the presence of her senior adviser, I advised her, in good faith, that they would break the Conference. She had strong views on the matter. She said that the Palestinians had shown solidarity to South Africa during her struggle against *apartheid* and that now South Africa must return that show of solidarity. I replied to the President that while

I understood her position, in my view she was about to break her own conference. The discussions were polite but intense. I went through the President's proposals line by line and made suggestions for language that I thought would keep the Conference together, while being faithful to a sense of justice.

By 5.00 am, the President had agreed to some re-drafts of her text, which she would distribute to delegations at 8.00 am that morning. But there was no typist available to re-type the document. I stepped into the breach and re-typed the two-page document, which the President duly circulated at 8.00 am. The President's proposals met with understanding on the part of the different regional groups of states. The scene was thus set for a successful conclusion of the Conference. When the final plenary session of the Conference convened, the various regional groups of delegations supported the President's proposals. But then, out of the blue, the Syrian representative proposed amendments that would have included harsher language. There was a major procedural debate on this with numerous points of order. I asked the Secretary of the meeting to give me his chair and performed the functions of the secretary of the meeting, advising the Chair on the handling of successive procedural challenges. In the end, the Syrian motion was not carried, and the Conference proceeded to the formal adoption of the DDPA.

I have described the foregoing events for a reason: the 1978 world conference had collapsed on the handling of the Palestinian situation, and the 2001 conference came within a hare's breath of collapsing also. This is to say that substantive human rights questions easily become overlaid by overt political challenges. This is something we need to bear in mind in future efforts for the implementation of the DDPA.

3.2 Vision Statements by All Countries

An insightful contribution of Mary Robinson, as Secretary-General of the Durban Conference, was to invite every participating government to adopt or update a national vision statement setting out the future hopes and aspirations of each country for policies of inclusiveness, tolerance and equality. With the assistance of the Irish Nobel Laureate in Literature, Seamus Heaney, Mary Robinson circulated the following statement to all participating governments in the Conference, which she signed, as did the venerable Nelson Mandela. She invited all Heads of State or Government to sign similarly.[20]

The document read as follows:

> **Tolerance and Diversity:**
> **A Vision for the 21st Century**
> As a new century begins, we believe each society needs to ask itself certain questions. Is it sufficiently inclusive? Is it non-discriminatory? Are norms of behaviour based on the principles enshrined in the Universal Declaration of Human Rights?

[20] For the text of the Vision Statement, see UN doc. WCR/IC/2001/Misc.3: Information paper, prepared for the Informal consultations of the Preparatory Committee, Geneva, 15–16 January 2001.

Racism, racial discrimination, xenophobia and all kinds of related intolerance have not gone away. We recognize that they persist in the new century and that their persistence is rooted in fear: fear of what is different, fear of the other, fear of the loss of personal security. And while we recognize that human fear is in itself ineradicable, we maintain that its consequences are not ineradicable.

We all constitute one human family. This truth has now become self-evident because of the first mapping of the human genome, an extraordinary achievement which not only reaffirms our common humanity but promises transformations in scientific thought and practice, as well as in the visions which our species can entertain for itself. It encourages us toward the full exercise of our human spirit, the reawakening of all its inventive, creative and moral capacities, enhanced by the equal participation of men and women. And it could make the twenty-first century an era of genuine fulfilment and peace.

We must strive to remind ourselves of this great possibility. Instead of allowing diversity of race and culture to become a limiting factor in human exchange and development, we must refocus our understanding, discern in such diversity the potential for mutual enrichment, and realize that it is the interchange between great traditions of human spirituality that offers the best prospect for the persistence of the human spirit itself. For too long such diversity has been treated as threat rather than gift. And too often that threat has been expressed in racial contempt and conflict, in exclusion, discrimination and intolerance.

Preparations for the *United Nations World Conference against Racism, Racial Discrimination, Xenophobia and Related Intolerance*, to be held in South Africa in September 2001, offer an opportunity to consider how far the aspirations of the three UN Decades Against Racism have been realized. The horrors of racism – from slavery to holocaust to apartheid to ethnic cleansing – have deeply wounded the victim and debased the perpetrator. These horrors are still with us in various forms. It is now time to confront them and to take comprehensive measures against them.

The World Conference should adopt a declaration and plan of action which would provide the standards, the structures, the remedies – in essence, the culture – to ensure full recognition of the dignity and equality of all, and full respect for their human rights.

Over the coming year we pledge ourselves to seek that conversion of mind and heart. What we envisage for every man, women and child is a life where the exercise of individual gifts and personal rights is affirmed by the dynamic solidarity of our membership of the one human family.

"Mary Robinson	Nelson Mandela	HoS or HoG"
[Signed]	[Signed]	[To be signed]

One of the tasks that could be undertaken in assessing the impact of the Durban Conference would be to take stock of whether governments have actually promoted and used national vision statements in their strategies for equality and non-discrimination. It would seem that not many countries have followed up on such vision statements.

4 Follow-Up Action

Shortly after the Durban Conference, we wrote and circulated to the staff of the Office of High Commissioner for Human Rights (OHCHR) the following *aide memoire* on the importance of implementation of the Durban Declaration and Programme of Action.

NOTE ON THE IMPLEMENTATION OF THE DURBAN DECLARATION AND PROGRAMME OF ACTION

1. In the aftermath of the Durban Conference, it is important to address the question of the responsibility of the United Nations Secretariat to support the continuing struggle against racism, racial discrimination, xenophobia and related intolerance. The Conference pointedly urged international organizations 'to contribute to the fight against racism, racial discrimination, xenophobia, and related intolerance.'
2. **Committee on the Elimination of Racial Discrimination (CERD)**: As the United Nations human rights programme has evolved, regular budget support for anti-discrimination activities now consists of part of the time of a single staff member to support the Committee on the Elimination of Racial Discrimination and modest *ad hoc* grants in support of the Decade against Racial Discrimination. The servicing of the Durban Conference, save for conference services, was largely achieved through the use of voluntary contributions.
3. The Conference specifically requested 'adequate resources for the Committee on the Elimination of Racial Discrimination in order to enable the full discharge of its mandate and stresses the importance of providing adequate resources for all United Nations human rights treaty bodies'.[21]
4. **Universal Ratification**: The Durban Conference made the assessment that 'countless human beings continue to the present day to be the victims of racism, racial discrimination, xenophobia and related intolerance'...[22] It affirmed that universal adherence and full implementation of the International Convention on the Elimination of All Forms of Racial Discrimination (ICERD) 'are of paramount importance for promoting equality and non-discrimination in the world'.[23] It set the goal of universal ratification of the Convention by the year 2005.[24]
5. It recommended that the Commission on Human Rights prepares complementary international standards to strengthen and update international instruments against racism racial discrimination, xenophobia and related intolerance in all their aspects.[25]
6. **Group protection**: The Conference called upon the United Nations to develop capacity-building programmes intended for Africans and people of African descent in the Americas and around the world.[26] It urged international organizations to address the situation of persons with disabilities who are also subject to racism and racial discrimination.[27] It encouraged the United Nations to promote and make use of the 'Guiding Principles on Internal Displacement', particularly those provisions relating to non-discrimination.[28]
7. **Data Collection and Research**: The Conference urged international organizations to improve data collection and analysis, to promote research, exchange of experiences and successful practices and develop promotional activities in this area; and to develop indicators of progress.[29] It further urged the United Nations to redress the marginalization of Africa's contribution to world history and civilization by developing and implementing a specific and comprehensive programme of research, education and mass

[21] DDPA, 2001, para 178.

[22] See Declaration.

[23] DDPA, para 77.

[24] Ibid para 75.

[25] Ibid para 199.

[26] Ibid para 6.

[27] Ibid para 57.

[28] Ibid para 65.

[29] Ibid para 93.

communication to disseminate widely a balanced and objective presentation of Africa's seminal contribution to humanity.[30]

8. The Conference invited the Office of the High Commissioner for Human Rights (OHCHR) to undertake regular consultations with NGOs and to encourage research activities aimed at collecting, maintaining and adapting the technical, scientific and information materials produced by all cultures around the world to fight racism.[31]
9. **Educational Programmes and Teaching Materials:** The Conference encouraged the United Nations to cooperate with states in initiating and developing cultural and educational programmes aimed at countering racism.[32] It urged the United Nations Educational, Scientific and Cultural Organisation (UNESCO) to provide support to States in preparation of teaching materials and tools.[33]
10. **Globalization:** The Conference encouraged international organizations to address those aspects of globalization which may lead to racism, racial discrimination, xenophobia and related intolerance.[34]
11. **Migrants:** The Conference called for OHCHR support to combat discrimination against migrant workers. It requested the OHCHR to pay special attention to violations of the human rights of victims of racism, racial discrimination, xenophobia and related intolerance, in particular migrants, including migrant workers to promote international cooperation in combatting xenophobia and, to this end, to develop programmes which can be applied in countries on the basis of appropriate cooperation programmes.[35]
12. **Trafficking:** The Conference recommended that the General Assembly consider declaring a United Nations year or decade against trafficking in persons, especially in women, youth and children in order to protect their dignity and human rights.[36]
13. **Technical Cooperation:** The Conference called upon states to assist OHCHR to develop and fund specific technical cooperation projects aimed at combating racism, racial discrimination, xenophobia and related intolerance.[37]
14. **Database:** The Conference recommended that OHCHR creates a database containing information on practical means to address racism, racial discrimination, xenophobia and related intolerance, including anti-discrimination legislation, as well as legal means to combat racial discrimination, on remedies available through international mechanisms; opportunities for technical cooperation; academic studies and specialized documentation.[38]
15. **Goodwill Ambassadors:** The Conference encouraged OHCHR to continue and expand the appointment of goodwill ambassadors in all countries of the world.[39] It called upon OHCHR to further increase awareness of the work of the Committee on the Elimination of Racial Discrimination.
16. **Indigenous People:** The Conference recommended that the United Nations Secretary-General conduct an evaluation of the results of the International Decade of the World's

[30] Ibid para 118.

[31] Ibid para 195.

[32] Ibid para 126.

[33] Ibid.

[34] Ibid para 152.

[35] Ibid para 196.

[36] Ibid para 201.

[37] Ibid para 197.

[38] Ibid para 191(d).

[39] Ibid para 193.

Indigenous People and make recommendations concerning how to mark the end of this decade, including an appropriate follow-up.[40]

17. **Third Decade:** The Conference urged the international community to support the activities of the Third Decade to Combat Racism and Racial Discrimination, which concludes in 2003.[41]
18. **Anti-Discrimination Unit:** The Conference supported the creation, within the Office of the High Commissioner, of an anti-discrimination unit to combat racism, racial discrimination, xenophobia and related intolerance, and invited the Office of the High Commissioner for Human Rights to consider the inclusion into its mandate, *inter alia*, the compilation of information on racial discrimination and its development, on legal and administrative support and advice to victims of racial discrimination, and the collection of background materials provided by States, international, regional and non-governmental organizations and national human rights institutions under the follow-up mechanism of the World Conference.[42]
19. **Eminent Persons:** In follow-up to the World Conference, the High Commissioner was requested to cooperate with five independent eminent experts to follow the implementation of the provisions of the Declaration and Programme of Action. An annual progress report to the Commission and the General Assembly would be part of the follow-up process.[43]
20. **Adequate Funding:** The Conference recognized that the success of the Programme of Action will require political will and adequate funding, and international cooperation.[44]

5 Conclusion

As this is written, we are approaching twenty-five years since the adoption of the Durban Declaration and Programme of Action. We will leave it to others to assess the extent to which the foregoing implementation measures were carried out. On item No. 12 above concerning trafficking in persons, we would note that when we performed the functions of UN High Commissioner for Human Rights, we called upon the Commission on Human Rights, at its annual session in 2004, to establish a Special Rapporteur against human trafficking. We drafted the resolution that the Commission adopted that same year establishing the post of Special Rapporteur against human trafficking. How effective the Special Rapporteur has been, will be also for others to assess. The Durban Conference was a historic event, and we were fortunate to have been part of its preparation and organization. Unfortunately, the scourges of racism and racial discrimination have not abated. On the contrary, they seem to have grown in magnitude.

In a political declaration to commemorate the twentieth anniversary of the adoption of the Durban Declaration and Programme of Action, the UN General Assembly

[40] Ibid para 203.

[41] Ibid para 200.

[42] Ibid para 191(c).

[43] Ibid para 191 (b).

[44] Ibid para 219. The original in the possession of the author.

acknowledged with deep concern a rise in discrimination, hate speech, stigmatization, racism, systemic racism, stereotypes, racial profiling, violence, xenophobia and intolerance, both in person and online, directed against, *inter alia,* Africans and people of African descent, Asians and people of Asian descent, indigenous peoples, Roma and persons belonging to other racial, ethnic, linguistic or religious minorities, as well as those motivated by prejudices against persons based on their religions or beliefs, such as, among others, Islamophobia, anti-Semitism and Christianophobia, and against women and children, migrants, refugees, forcibly displaced persons, asylum-seekers, internally displaced persons, persons with disabilities, older persons, youth and other persons in vulnerable situations.[45]

As the world marks the culmination of the first quarter of this century, it will undoubtedly evaluate the legacy of Durban to the challenges of inequalities and racial injustices in these times. And it will need to tackle the epochal changes of our times and the related challenges of protecting people at risk.

References

Committee on the Elimination of Racial Discrimination and the progress made towards the achievement of the objectives of the International Convention on the Elimination of All Forms of Racial Discrimination: Published on the occasion of the World Conference to Combat Racism and Racial Discrimination, Geneva, 14–25 August 1978. United Nations publication, Sales No. E.79.XIV.4, New York, 1970

Information paper, prepared for the Informal consultations of the Preparatory Committee, Geneva, 15–16 January 2001. UN doc. WCR/IC/2001/Misc.3

Report of the Seminar on Recourse Procedures Available to Victims of Racism and Racial Discrimination and Activities Undertaken at the Regional Level, Geneva 9–20 July 1979. UN doc. ST/HR/SER.A/3, United Nations. New York, 1979. Accessed 13 June 2025

Round Table of University Professors and Directors of Race Relations Institutions on the Teaching of Problems of Racial Discrimination, Geneva, 5–9 November 1979. UN doc. ST/HR/SER.A/5, United Nations, Geneva, 1979. Accessed 13 June 2025

Santa Cruz, Hernán, Racial Discrimination Study: Revised and Updated Version, Special Rapporteur of the Sub-Commission on Prevention of Discrimination and Protection of Minorities, 1976. UN publication, Sales No.E.76.XIV.2. Discrimination raciale: Accessed 13 June 2025

[45] General Assembly resolution 76/1, 22 September 2021, para. 7.

Procedural Issues at the Durban Conference Against Racism

Marc Bossuyt

1 Introduction

International protection of human rights is first a matter of defining international norms and setting up international systems of monitoring respect for those norms. The process of negotiating the adoption of such norms and systems takes place in political fora. The General Assembly and its Third Committee (dealing with Human Rights), the Human Rights Council, and Human Rights World Conferences are such political fora by excellence. Such processes are governed by procedural rules, which play a prominent role when political tensions between the negotiators are high. Provisional rules of procedure were adopted for the Durban Conference during the first session of the preparatory committee.[1] This chapter illustrates the importance of procedural issues by analysing the discussions at the 2001 World Conference

Prof. Em. Marc Bossuyt, Chairperson/Rapporteur of the Working Group on the (Durban) Draft Declaration.
Revised and Republished based on Bossuyt, Marc, "Procedural Confusion at the Main Committee of the Durban Conference against Racism", *Human Rights Monitor,* 2001/56, pp. 12–15, and *International Human Rights Protection: Balanced, Critical, Realistic,* Cambridge, Intersentia, 2016, pp. 91–101.

[1] A/CONF.189/2 (14 August 2001), adopted on 31 August 2001. They remained the operative standard throughout the conference. Available on: https://documents.un.org/doc/undoc/gen/g01/154/73/pdf/g0115473.pdf.

M. Bossuyt (✉)
University of Antwerp, Antwerp, Belgium

C. S. Namakula (ed.), *Untold Reflections from the World Conference Against Racism*, SpringerBriefs in Law, https://doi.org/10.1007/978-3-032-17265-5_2

against Racism, Racial Discrimination, Xenophobia and Related Intolerance in detail.[2]

The conference was scheduled to come to an end on the evening of Friday 7 September 2001, but as neither the Working Groups nor the Facilitators to whom some particular "difficult issues" had been entrusted could finish their work in time, the Conference lasted one day longer. In the early morning of Saturday 8 September 2001, the two Working Groups, one on the draft declaration and one on the draft programme of action, resumed their work from 7 am to 10 am. Soon after the closure of the Working Groups' last meeting, the Drafting Committee, chaired by Ambassador Ali Khorram (Islamic Republic of Iran), started with the adoption of its report based on the brief reports transmitted to him by the Chairpersons/Rapporteurs of the two Working Groups.[3] It is important to note that all those organs (the two Working Groups, the Drafting Committee, the Main Committee and the Conference) were plenary organs in which the 171 participating States were represented.

Once the report of the Drafting Committee was adopted, it was presented to the Main Committee. Three so-called difficult issues remained to be solved. Those issues related to (1) the grounds of discrimination, (2) the Middle East, and (3) the Past, which included the questions of slavery and colonialism. They had been entrusted to Facilitators who tried to agree on a consensus language, which would be a substitute for the paragraphs in the draft declaration and in the draft programme of action concerning those issues.

Besides the paragraphs relating to the "difficult issues", only a few paragraphs were still ongoing at the level of the Working Groups when they concluded their work.[4] Some of those paragraphs belonged to a few upon which there was no agreement as to whether they belonged to the category of paragraphs that would be substituted by those on which the Facilitators should try to reach a general agreement.

[2] The official report of the World Conference against Racism, Racial Discrimination, Xenophobia and Related Intolerance has been published as document A/CONF.189/12 (Part I–III). For the Report of the Main Committee, see *ibid.*, Part II, pp. 25–32. The present analysis is mainly based on the videos of the meetings of the Main Committee which may be consulted on internet: www.un.org/WCAR/webcast/0908/-maincomittee/smil. The text of the Declaration and the Programme of Action is available on www.unhchr.ch/htlm/racism.

[3] The Working Group on the draft declaration was chaired by Professor Marc Bossuyt (Belgium) and the Working Group on the draft programme of action by Ambassador Bonaventure Bowa (Zambia).

[4] As far as the more than 160 paragraphs of the Durban Declaration are concerned, 15% of those paragraphs were adopted during the second session of the Preparatory Committee, 31% during its third session, 40% by the Working Group in Durban and 13% were the result of the work of the Facilitators to whom the "difficult issues" were entrusted. From the paragraphs not entrusted to them, only four contained language between brackets when the Working Group had to stop its work at 10 a.m. of 8 September.

This was particularly the case with preambular paragraph 30[5] and operative paragraph 33[6] of the draft declaration. Those paragraphs related to foreign occupation in wording that was considered by some delegations to be generic in nature, and by others as referring to the situation in the Middle East.

On the assumption that the Facilitators would come up with wording that would substitute the paragraphs relating to the difficult issues, the only remaining issue was the fate of those few other paragraphs on which the Working Groups had not been able to reach a general agreement. Was it possible, in the final stage of the Conference, to reopen the discussion on those paragraphs or was deletion of the ongoing paragraphs or, at least, of all words kept between square brackets the only way out?

2 Procedure Before the Main Committee (First Part)

The first part of the Main Committee consisted of four meetings separated by successive suspensions.

2.1 The First Meeting

Among the many interventions made during the first meeting of the first part of the Main Committee, chaired by Ambassador Claudio Moreno (Italy), four delegations enquired about the status of the remaining paragraphs on which no consensus could be reached. In reply to successive questions on this matter from representatives of Iran, Pakistan and Kenya, the executive secretary of the Conference, Mr Singh, indicated that there was no clear answer to those questions and that a referral of those issues to the next session of the Commission on Human Rights could be a way

[5] The draft preambular paragraph 30 read as follows: "[*Reaffirming* that colonization by settlers and foreign occupation constitute sources, causes and forms of racism, racial discrimination, xenophobia and related intolerance]". An alternative wording had been suggested in the Working Group on the draft declaration on which it had also been impossible to reach a general agreement: "Reaffirming/*Affirming* that [colonization/settlers colonization] of an occupied territory in violation of article 49 of the 4th Geneva Convention of 1949 *creates a situation conducive to* forms of racism, racial discrimination, xenophobia and related intolerance". Those drafts had been taken up for discussion by the Working Group on the draft declaration on the very morning of 8 September, but without success.

[6] The draft operative paragraph 33 read as follows: "We affirm that a foreign occupation founded on settlements, its laws based on racial discrimination, with the aim of continuing domination of the occupied territory, as well as its practices which consist of reinforcing a total military blockade, isolating towns, cities and villages under occupation from each other, totally contradict the purposes and principles of the Charter of the United Nations and constitutes a serious violation of international human rights and humanitarian law, a new kind of apartheid, a crime against humanity and a serious threat to international peace and security".

out. Shortly after the arrival of the President of the Conference, Dr Zuma (South Africa), at the Main Committee, the representative of the United Arab Emirates expressed his "dismay and shock" that the "generic" paragraphs were not discussed. He considered this to be "unfair and unacceptable". The Chairperson of the Main Committee took note of this statement.

Soon afterwards, Dr Zuma informed the Main Committee of the general agreement reached on the paragraphs concerning the Past and the Middle East. The adoption of those paragraphs, without a vote, was welcomed by applause. Further interventions on diverse issues were referred to the plenary by the Chairperson. When several delegations insisted on asking for the floor, the Chairperson suspended the meeting.

2.2 *The Second Meeting*

When the meeting resumed, the representative of Qatar made a rather long statement on behalf of the Organisation of the Islamic Conference (OIC). In this statement, he complained about a distorting and misleading media campaign orchestrated against his group. While welcoming the recognition of the inalienable right of the Palestinian people to the establishment of an independent state, he regretted the failure to condemn the discriminatory policies of Israel.

Immediately afterwards, the representative of Syria requested support for the adoption of the remaining paragraphs relating to the question of foreign occupation. This request was supported by Pakistan and Egypt, while Canada, supported by Belgium, on behalf of the Member States of the European Union, and Australia, rejected any re-negotiation. After the representative of Iran had stated that those "general" paragraphs, which, in his opinion, were discriminated against, should not be deferred again to a later stage, the Chairperson suspended the meeting for an exchange of ideas by the regional coordinators on the continuation of the work.

2.3 *The Third Meeting*

After the second suspension of the meeting, the Chairperson read out the wording of the paragraph on the grounds of discrimination,[7] which was then adopted by general agreement. With respect to the other outstanding paragraphs, on the contrary, he announced that, despite a meeting at the highest level, there was no consen-

[7] The final wording of this paragraph reads as follows: "*Recognizes* that racism, racial discrimination, xenophobia and related intolerance occur on the grounds of race, colour, descent or national or ethnic origin and that victims suffer multiple or aggravated forms of discrimination based on other related grounds such as sex, language, religion, political or other opinion, social origin, property, birth or other status". This is a substitute for wording that would have enlarged the enumera-

sus for a political solution. He therefore recurred to the advice of the representative of the Legal Counsel.

Twice the representative of the Legal Counsel explained that the Conference could not adopt bracketed text and that the Main Committee could not delete the brackets or retain the language without a decision of the Main Committee, nor maintain the brackets, the consequence being deleting the language, without a decision of the Main Committee. Twice the Chairperson "adopted" the "solution" forwarded by the representative of the Legal Counsel. Twice the representative of Pakistan intervened to enquire whether there was a consensus for deletion or keeping the brackets. Invoking time constraints, the Chairperson adjourned the meeting.

2.4 The Fourth Meeting

After the third suspension of the meeting, the Chairperson stated that under the ruling of the President of the Conference, he had to resume the meeting of the Main Committee. He stated that the Committee had listened to and accepted the advice of the Legal Counsel to the effect that the Committee addresses the issue of the paragraphs which were in brackets. He proposed to proceed on the basis that unless there was a request to discuss those paragraphs, they would be deleted.

The Minister of Foreign Affairs of Syria insisted on reaching a consensus on the paragraphs concerning foreign occupation, in the absence of which he would ask for a vote. Invoking a lack of time and of interpretation facilities, the Chairperson stated that the Committee had to go straight to a vote.

On behalf of the European Union, the Minister of Justice of Belgium, requested to avoid a vote at all costs and appealed to the Committee to concentrate on the text on which there was consensus. The representative of Pakistan also considered that this was not the time for a vote, and she proposed that the Drafting Committee meets for one or two hours to discuss those paragraphs which, as she stated, were never discussed. In support of Pakistan, the representative of Malaysia stated that there would have been no request for a vote if proper consultations had taken place; this assertion was denied by those delegations that were asking for 'consensus now'. The representative of Malaysia emphasised that the vote had been requested on the paragraphs proposed by Syria but not on the presidential text relating to the Middle East.

When the Chairperson announced that he would adjourn the meeting for an exchange of views with the Presidency of the Conference, the representative of Brazil asked the floor to join the appeal made on behalf of the European Union while revealing that, irrespective of the substance of those paragraphs, he had firm instructions to vote against, if they would be put to the vote. After the representative

tion of the Universal Declaration of Human Rights with grounds such as gender, disability, age, HIV/AIDS or other health conditions, sexual orientation and work.

of Canada had also asked not to go to a vote on those paragraphs which had been raised in the Working Groups and in the sessions of the Preparatory Committee giving rise to strong objections, the Chairperson adjourned the meeting.

3 Procedure Before the Main Committee (Second Part)

After yet another suspension, which lasted more than two hours, the second part of the Main Committee was chaired by one of its vice-chairpersons: Ambassador Alexander Slabi (Czech Republic).

3.1 The Appeal of the President of the Conference

At the start of the second part of the final meeting of the Main Committee, Dr Zuma, the President of the Conference, made, as she said, a last appeal, which was followed by loud applause: "This was not going to be an easy Conference. We are running out of time, but can we, who have worked so hard, at the end not come to any conclusion?". The Chairperson then proposed that everything which had not been accepted, be put aside.

The Minister of Foreign Affairs of Syria, however, referred to new language[8] for preambular paragraph 30 and operative paragraph 33 of the draft declaration, which, according to him, had been suggested by the President of the Conference. The representative of Pakistan stated that, if "putting aside" would mean that those paragraphs would not be retained in the final document without discussion, she could not accept the proposal of the Chairperson. She affirmed that the European Union had given assurances that those paragraphs should be dealt with once there was a solution on the paragraphs relating to the Middle East.[9] Taking the floor, two more times, she insisted that the Committee should first take a decision on the proposal made by Syria, before dealing with the proposal of the Chairperson to put all non-consensus text aside. The same position was taken by the United Arab Emirates, while Belgium, on behalf of the European Union, supported by the Russian

[8] The wording referred to by the Minister of Foreign Affairs of Syria read as follows:

- Preambular para. 30 "*Reaffirming* that foreign occupation contrary to international law can result in conditions that give rise to racism, racial discrimination, xenophobia and related intolerance."
- Operative para. 33: "We reaffirm that foreign occupation contrary to the principles and purposes of the Charter of the United Nations is a threat to international peace and security".

[9] As a matter of fact, those paragraphs belonged precisely to the category of a few paragraphs on which Pakistan, on behalf of the Islamic States, and Canada, on behalf of the Western Group, had been unable to agree as to the question whether they should be substituted or not by the paragraphs on the Middle East.

Federation and Brazil, considered that the proposal of the Chairperson should be dealt with first.

After one more intervention by Pakistan and three interventions by Syria, that kept referring to wording offered by the President of the Conference, the Chairperson stated that, as during the two-hour break "nothing happened or maybe something happened, but the result was nothing", the new text referred to by Syria was not submitted properly. Accordingly, his own proposal was the only one officially raised.

3.2 The No Action Motion

When the Chairperson of the Main Committee announced his intention to make a ruling under Rule 21 of the Rules of Procedure,[10] Brazil asked for the floor on a point of order to make a formal "no action motion", under Rule 44.3 of the Rules of Procedure,[11] on all remaining paragraphs not considered by the Working Groups. The Chairperson interpreted the no action motion of Brazil as a motion of adjournment of the debate under Rule 26 of the Rules of Procedure[12] and announced that he would give the floor to two representatives in favour and two opposing the motion. The first speaker on the issue was the representative of Algeria, who complained about a degree of lightness or frivolity with the Rules of Procedure and requested the Chairperson to explain whether his proposal "which was considered favourably by Syria, was a substitute that would enable the Committee to respond favourably to the appeal of Dr Zuma".[13] The second speaker was the Minister of Foreign Affairs

[10] Rule 21: "During the discussion of any matter, a representative of a State may at any time raise a point of order, which shall be immediately decided by the President in accordance with these rules. A representative may appeal against the ruling of the President. The appeal shall be immediately put to the vote, and the President's ruling shall stand unless overruled by a majority of the representatives present and voting. A representative may not, in raising a point of order, speak on the substance of the matter under discussion". The Rules of Procedure of the World Conference appear in document A.CONF.189/2 (14 August 2001).

[11] "A motion requiring that no decision be taken on a proposal shall be put to the vote before a vote is taken on the proposal in question". The text of this third paragraph of Rule 44 is analogous to the well-known Rule 65.2 of the Rules of Procedure of the functional commissions of the Economic and Social Council (E/5975/Rev.1, 1994): "A motion requiring that no decision be taken on a proposal shall have priority over that proposal".

[12] Rule 26: "A representative of any State participating in the Conference may at any time move the adjournment of the debate on the question under discussion. Permission to speak on the motion shall be accorded to only two representatives in favour of and two opposing the adjournment, after which the motion shall, subject to Rule 29, be immediately put to the vote".

[13] From this and the two later interventions made by Algeria, it appears that the proposal referred to by Syria as the President's (Dr Zuma's informal) proposal was considered by some as a proposal made by the Chairperson of the Main Committee.

of Syria who said that one should either accept the proposal referred to as Dr Zuma's proposal[14] or his original proposal.[15]

The Chairperson interpreted the statements by Algeria and Syria as opposing the motion and asked whether another representative wanted to speak in favour of the motion. The representative of New Zealand spoke in favour of the Brazilian motion. The representative of Iran expressed great frustration at the way the Chairperson conducted the work of the Committee stating that the first proposal came from Syria and should be acted upon first. The Chairperson called upon the representative of the Legal Counsel for clarification of the Rules of Procedure.

3.3 The Representative of the Legal Counsel

In a rather long intervention, the representative of the Legal Counsel referred first to Rule 44.1, 1st sentence, according to which "[i]f two or more proposals, other than amendments, relate to the same question, they shall, unless the Conference decides otherwise, be voted on in the order in which they were submitted".[16] This would apply to the original Syrian proposal and to the proposal of the Chairperson. However, the Main Committee was now confronted with a no action motion, in accordance with Rule 44.3, on Syria's proposal having precedence over action on that proposal.[17] According to the representative of the Legal Counsel—and as was stated by the Chairperson—a "no action motion" is to be dealt with in accordance with Rule 26.[18] Accordingly, permission to speak on the motion should be accorded to only two representatives in favour and two opposing, after which the motion should be immediately put to a vote.

The representative of Pakistan did agree with this reading of the Rules of Procedure, but she contested that anyone had spoken in favour or against the Brazilian proposal. The Chairperson replied that Algeria and Syria had not contradicted him when he considered their interventions as opposing the motion. The representative of Algeria reacted very forcefully. He did not allow the Chairperson to interpret his words wrongly and said that he would challenge the Chairperson if he would continue that kind of game. Apparently intimidated by this unusual personal attack, the Chairperson asked whether Brazil insisted on its motion.

Stating that he only wanted to provide an opportunity for a way out, the representative of Brazil withdrew its motion as only one delegation had spoken in favour of it. This withdrawal was met with applause. However, the representative of the

[14] *Cf. supra* note 8.

[15] *Cf. supra* notes 5 and 6.

[16] The text of this first sentence of the first paragraph is identical to the first sentence of Rule 65.1 of the above-mentioned Rules of Procedure of the functional commissions of ECOSOC.

[17] *Cf. supra* note 11.

[18] *Cf. supra* note 12.

Russian Federation intervened immediately to state that he had raised his nameplate on several occasions to give support for the Brazilian motion and the Minister of Justice of Belgium, on behalf of the European Union, reintroduced the Brazilian no action motion.[19]

Consequently, the Chairperson returned to the procedure provided for in Rule 26. The representative of Argentina stated that he had also tried, with no success, to ask for the floor to support Brazil. The representative of the Russian Federation supported the (now) Belgian no action motion, which was opposed by the representative of Syria and, surprisingly, by the representative of South Africa, who stated, under applause, that he could not support postponing discussion on any matter or on this matter in particular.

3.4 The Vote on the No Action Motion

After a request for clarification concerning the object of the vote, from the representatives of India and China, was met by the Chairperson in reading out Rule 26 once again, a roll call vote took place at the request of the representative of Australia. The result of the vote was 51 votes to 37, with 11 abstentions and astonishingly 70 absent or not participating in the vote.[20] According to Rule 36 of the Rules of Procedure,[21] the Belgian "no action motion", a matter of procedure requiring a simple majority,[22] was adopted. After some brief interventions by a few delegations, mainly explaining their vote, the Chairperson concluded the work of the Main Committee by stating that the texts that had already been adopted went to the plenary.

---

[19] In doing so, Brazil and Belgium applied Rule 31 of the Rules of Procedure: "A proposal or a motion may be withdrawn by its sponsor at any time before voting on it has commenced, provided that it has not been amended. A proposal or a motion thus withdrawn may be reintroduced by any representative".

[20] Voted in favour: 23 Western States, 12 Latin-American States, 11 Eastern European States, 3 African States (Gabon, Ghana and the Democratic Republic Congo) and 2 Asian States (Fiji and Japan); voted against: 19 Asian States, 14 African States and 4 Caribbean States; abstained: 4 African States (Kenya, Senegal, Seychelles and Togo), 3 Asian States (India, Philippines, Singapore), 3 Eastern European States (Armenia, Azerbaijan and Bosnia-Herzegovina) and 1 Latin-American State (Ecuador). Most impressive was the high number of States absent or not participating in the vote: 30 African States, 14 Asian States, 11 Latin American or Caribbean States, 11 Eastern European States and even 4 Western States (Andorra, Greece, Iceland and Malta).

[21] Rule 36: "1. Subject to Rule 34 ['The Conference shall exert all possible efforts to ensure that its work and the adoption of its report are accomplished by general agreement'], decisions of the Conference on all matters of substance shall be taken by a two-thirds majority of the representatives present and voting. 2. Unless the Conference decides otherwise and except as otherwise provided, decisions of the Conference on all matters of procedure shall be taken by a simple majority of the representatives present and voting".

[22] The adoption of the Syrian proposals, a matter of substance, would have required a two-third majority.

4 Conclusion

The debates at the Main Committee were characterised by a lot of confusion. This was due, at least as far as some of the key players are concerned, to a) a lack of knowledge of the Rules of Procedure; b) a lack of experience with procedural debates; c) lack of time; d) lack of coordination within and among regional groups; and e) lack of flexibility in the decision-making process within some groups, which would have wanted a suspension for consultations before any procedural move. All this was aggravated by a) the physical and mental exhaustion of many delegates at the end of a very tiring conference, b) the frustration of several delegations, which felt that they had given in too much or obtained too little and c) by the setting in the Conference room which was unfit for a major procedural battle. The Chairperson, as well as the members of the Secretariat assisting him, could in many instances neither see the nameplates of the delegations nor distinguish which delegations asked for the floor and in what order. While most of the formal conference proceedings had taken place within two working groups in which the delegations got used to work with each other during long days and under a stable chairperson, the final debate took place among actors who were not acquainted with working together.

An analysis of the records reveals an accumulation of misunderstandings, as for instance, a) between the text of the agreement on the Middle East and on the Past proposed by Dr Zuma and the bracketed paragraphs proposed by Syria; b) between the proposal of the Chairperson of the Main Committee (Ambassador Slabi) to delete the bracketed paragraphs and the informal proposal made by the President of the Conference (Dr Zuma) in replacement of the bracketed paragraphs proposed by Syria; c) between the said proposal of the Chairperson of the Main Committee and the no action motion proposed by Brazil (and reintroduced by Belgium) and d) between the no action motion under Rule 43.3 of the Rules of Procedure and a motion of adjournment of the debate under Rule 26 of the Rules of Procedure. There was also confusion as to the, nonetheless, clear intervention of the representative of the Legal Counsel on the need for a decision by the Main Committee to delete the brackets or to delete the bracketed text and as to whether the no action motion was related to the bracketed paragraphs proposed by Syria or to all bracketed paragraphs of the draft declaration and the draft programme of action.

While undoubtedly the great majority of the delegations disliked having a vote taken at the end of the Conference, it could not be avoided, due to the insistence of the Minister of Foreign Affairs of Syria. Despite the great number of delegations absent or not participating in the vote or rather due to this unusual great number of delegations not present or not voting, the majority was sufficiently great (51 against 37) to discourage any attempt by the minority to press for further votes. This allowed the Chairperson of the Main Committee to put an end to the proceedings of the Main Committee and the President of the Conference could, after a brief suspension, proceed to the adoption of the Durban Declaration and the Programme of Action

(DDPA) without a vote.[23] The adoption of the Declaration and the Programme of Action was followed by a long series of declarations and statements which are reproduced in the Report of the World Conference.[24] The outcome of the Conference lost much of the attention it deserved when three days later (on September 11, 2001) two planes flew into the Twin Towers in New York.

References

Bossuyt M, "Procedural Confusion at the Main Committee of the Durban Conference against Racism", Human Rights Monitor, 2001/56, pp 12–15, and International Human Rights Protection: Balanced, Critical, Realistic. Cambridge, Intersentia, 2016, pp 91–101

Report of the World Conference against Racism, Racial Discrimination, Xenophobia and Related Intolerance has been published as document A/CONF.189/12

Rules of Procedure of the functional commissions of the Economic and Social Council (E/5975/Rev.1, 1994)

Rules of Procedure of the World Conference against Racism, A.CONF.189/2 (14 August 2001)

[23] The difficulties that arose later to the precise location in the Declaration and the Programme of Action of some of the paragraphs of the agreement on the Past, were unrelated to the discussion which had taken place in the Main Committee. Those difficulties could have been avoided, if the paragraphs of the agreement had been sent in the early morning of the last day of the Conference to the two Working Groups. Indeed, both Working Groups held their last meeting on Saturday 8 September from 7 a.m. to 10 a.m. There would have been no ambiguity on the question whether some paragraphs belonged either to the Declaration or to the Programme of Action or to both texts, if they had been sent to the Working Groups for inclusion in their respective drafts.

[24] See the declarations made by Australia, Belgium, Canada, Chile, Ecuador, Iran, Syria and Switzerland as well as the statements that were intended to be made by Barbados, Guatemala, Japan, Latvia, New Zealand, Trinidad and Tobago, and Turkey before and by Brazil, China, Iraq, Mexico, Qatar, the United Arab Emirates and Venezuela after the adoption of the Declaration and the Programme of Action and the statements made at the closure of the Conference on behalf of the regional groups by Kenya, India, Slovakia, Mexico and Belgium (A/CONF.189/12 (Part II), pp. 38–63).

An Inside View of the Durban World Conference Against Racism

Marc Bossuyt

In Memory of José Augusto Lindgren Alves (1946–2022)

1 Criticism Against the Durban Conference

According to Michael Banton,[1] a former British member of the UN Committee on the Elimination of Racial Discrimination (CERD), a senior UN official described the first World Conference against Racism (1978) as a "disaster" and the second World Conference (1983) as a "non-event". The first Conference, from which the Western delegations withdrew, as well as the second Conference, which resulted in the adoption of the declaration by a vote (101 against 12) were held in Geneva. In Michael Banton's view, the third Conference (in Durban in 2001) was "a calamity that has damaged the reputation of the UN". In his language, "the conference may well have done more harm than good. It used up much time, money, and energy for little benefit; many governments treated the conference as a political arena in which they sought to impose additional responsibilities on other states without accepting any themselves".[2]

Of all criticism against the Durban Conference, Ambassador José Augusto Lindgren Alves (Brazil), a member of CERD (Committee on the Elimination of

Prof. Em. Marc Bossuyt, Chairperson/Rapporteur of the Working Group on the (Durban) Draft Declaration.

[1] Banton (2002), p. 356.

[2] *Ibid* p. 360.

M. Bossuyt (✉)
University of Antwerp, Antwerp, Belgium

C. S. Namakula (ed.), *Untold Reflections from the World Conference Against Racism*, SpringerBriefs in Law, https://doi.org/10.1007/978-3-032-17265-5_3

Racial Discrimination) from 2002 till 2017, was most shocked by the one made by Professor Banton. In his opinion, "Professor Banton criticised the conference as if it were an autonomous entity, capable of acting beyond the will of its participants and isolated from the world context in which it took place. He seems not to realize that 'calamity' was not the Conference itself, but the 'circumstance' under which it was finally convened, very different from the one under which it was devised". Ambassador Lindgren concluded that "In spite of all its defects, Durban was indeed the best conference that could have occurred on such comprehensive and delicate themes, under such adverse circumstances".[3]

When he was a member of the UN Sub-Commission on the Prevention of Discrimination and the Protection of Minorities, Ambassador Lindgren had taken the initiative to propose the convening of a World Conference against Racism on 4 August 1994.[4] To that effect, resolution 1994/2 of the Sub-Commission[5] was adopted by consensus on 12 August 1994.[6] As a colleague of Ambassador Lindgren, I was one of the 23 co-authors of that resolution.[7] In his evaluation of the World Conference in 2002, he was very critical of the attitude of the Western European and Others Group (WEOG)[8] thus "what had not been expected was their radical inflexibility, and their frequent obstruction to even the simplest paragraphs, on virtually every subject. […] In Durban, the Western Group assumed 'byzantine' positions, proposing irrelevant changes to the most unimportant texts… [T]he rigidity and provocative attitudes of Western countries engendered the feeling that the whole exercise of negotiations was hopeless".[9]

---

[3] In italics in the original text. Lindgren Alves (2003), pp. 383–384. Among those "adverse circumstances", the author mentions the following "contemporary forms of intolerance": aggression against immigrants in Europe; resurgence of white supremacist doctrines in the US; the genocide in Rwanda; aggravated Asian ethnic-religious conflicts; hooliganism of skinheads and neo-Nazi groups; ethnic cleansing and bloody wars; the electoral growth of populist far-right parties (*ibid.*, p. 364).

[4] E/CN.4/Sub.2/1994/SR.6, §28.

[5] Entitled: "A world conference against racism, racial and ethnic discrimination, xenophobia and other related contemporary forms of intolerance".

[6] E/CN.4/Sub.2/1994/SR.17, §122.

[7] E/CN.4/Sub.2/1994/56, §100.

[8] Comprising of 29 UN members: Andorra, Australia, Austria, Belgium, Canada, Denmark, Finland, France, Germany, Greece, Iceland, Ireland, Israel, Italy, Liechtenstein, Luxembourg, Malta, Monaco, Netherlands, New Zealand, Norway, Portugal, San Marino, Spain, Sweden, Switzerland, Turkey, United Kingdom, United States of America.

[9] Lindgren Alves, *op. cit.*, pp. 369–370.

2 The Working Group on the Draft Declaration

In a footnote,[10] Ambassador Lindgren made exception for "the extraordinary work of Belgium". The Durban Conference was preceded by regional conferences held in Strasbourg (11–13 October 2000), Santiago de Chile (5–7 December 2000), Dakar (22–24 January 2001) and Teheran (19–21 February 2001). It was prepared in Geneva by three sessions (1–5 May 2000; 1 May–1 June 2001; and 31 July–10 August 2001) of a Preparatory Committee. From the second session onward, this "Prep. Com." established two plenary Working Groups: one on the draft Declaration and another on the draft Programme of Action, chaired by Ambassador Patrick Hénault (France) and by Ambassador Gilberto Vergne Saboia (Brazil) respectively. Progress in Geneva was very slow. Normally, most of the texts to be adopted at an international conference are agreed upon before the Conference is held. For the Durban conference, only 40% of the paragraphs of the draft Declaration was adopted in Geneva during the second and the third sessions of the "Prep. Com." The WEOG was very sceptical of the chances of success of the Conference.

The Durban Conference was attended by many leaders of the developing world with Fidel Castro of Cuba and Yasser Arafat of Palestine as the most remarkable. Louis Michel, Minister for Foreign Affairs of Belgium presiding over the EU delegation, was one of the few Ministers for Foreign Affairs of an EU-Member State in attendance. Before the start of the Conference, Patrick Hénault, the French Ambassador for Human Rights, had indicated that he did not want to serve as Chairperson of the Working Group on the draft Declaration anymore. He did not expect that a positive outcome of the Conference was likely. Inquiries with other Western delegations to find a replacement were not successful. Nobody wanted to be associated with a probable failure. However, at the WEOG meeting before the opening of the Conference, the French delegation announced that at the insistence of many Western delegations, Ambassador Hénault would accept that task, "provided that" he would resign if no sensible progress could be made.

2.1 Election of the Chairperson of the Working Group on the Draft Declaration

Great was my surprise when a few hours later I was requested to immediately join the main building where the Conference was held, to be elected as chairperson of the Working Group on the draft Declaration. The WEOG proposal to entrust the chair of that Working Group to Ambassador Hénault conditionally had been rejected by the General Committee. That General Committee was composed of the President of the Conference (Dr Zuma, South Africa), 21 Vice-Presidents and the Rapporteur General (Ms Edna Maria Santos Roland, Brazil). On the recommendation of the

[10] *Ibid.,* p. 370, note 13.

Belgian Permanent Representative in Geneva (Ambassador Jean-Marie Noirfalisse), Minister Louis Michel had nominated me. The Deputy UN High Commissioner for Human Rights Bertie Ramcharan had assured the UN High Commissioner for Human Rights, Mrs Mary Robinson, that considering the way I had chaired the UN Commission on Human Rights in 1989, I could be entrusted with that task.

In his evaluation, Ambassador Lindgren[11] was kind enough to state that I had chaired that Working Group "with ability and dedication". An observer at the conference, Chip Pitts,[12] referred to "the able leadership of Professor Marc Bossuyt of Belgium. ... His approach to dealing with political manoeuvres [...] was generally to be scrupulously fair [...] (except in the most egregious or offensive attempts, which he would often deal with using humour or quick logic)". He added that "Bossuyt's insights as to lessons learned from the conference would undoubtedly be of value for such conferences, and the human rights community would be well-served if he could be persuaded to document drafting principles to be kept in mind for future reference".[13] When I reflected upon my chairmanship six years later,[14] I summarized my approach as follows: "Applying endless patience, strict neutrality, all the procedural tricks proper to UN meetings and some occasional humour". That experience constituted for me the most hectic nine days of my professional life. I seize the present opportunity to explain in somewhat more detail my approach to that chairmanship.[15]

2.1.1 Confidence Building

The first objective in starting my chairmanship was trying to gain the confidence of the 169 delegations constituting the Working Group. I am a Belgian citizen and as such I was a member of the Belgian delegation, one of the (then 15) Member States of the European Union. It was helpful that I was not a professional diplomat, but a university professor, a constitutional judge and, as a member of the Committee on the Elimination of Racial Discrimination, a UN independent expert. I was careful to deal with all delegations in an even-handed and fair manner. I gave them an equal opportunity to present their views. Making abstraction of my own views, I approached all proposals without pre-conceived sentiments. Only when a proposal did not make sense, I dared to show some reservation encouraging thus delegations to speak out against it. Progressively, I tried from time to time to disarm some unhelpful proposals, substantive or procedural, by "some occasional humour". Humour is risky in an international environment with participants of different

[11] Lindgren Alves, *op. cit.*, p. 370.

[12] Pitts (an international lawyer of Dallas who attended the Conference on behalf of the International Service for Human Rights) (2001), pp. 15–23.

[13] *Ibid* pp. 16 and 21.

[14] Bossuyt (2016a), pp. 195–196.

[15] Previously, I had already the opportunity to write about substantive aspects of the Conference, see Bossuyt and Vandeginste (2001), pp. 341–350.

cultural backgrounds. The ever-present need for translation in different languages increases the risk of misunderstandings. Humour can be a helpful tool, but it must be used sparingly.

It is of the utmost importance for a chairperson of a diplomatic conference to keep a panoramic eye on what happens in the room. There are always movements going on, and the chairperson must watch them attentively. He can learn a lot by watching the visual expression of the participants. Who looks happy? Who looks unhappy or even angry? Who looks indifferent or puzzled or nervous? Who is leaving his seat to talk with whom? The chairperson may not get lost in studying documents and should avoid as much as possible to be distracted by whoever tries to speak privately with him during a meeting. Observing what happens in the meeting room helps to be prepared for upcoming problems. It is also important to clearly explain, before proposing a decision to be taken, what its subject is, and what will be the effect of its adoption. Any ambiguity in the adoption of a decision can cost precious time afterwards. A good example of this is the controversy about the location of paragraphs in the Declaration and the Programme of Action. Due to this controversy, the final texts of the Durban World Conference could not be made available before January 2002, months after the end of the Conference.

2.1.2 Facilitators

One of the techniques used while dealing with specific paragraphs was to suspend the discussion by appointing a facilitator among the participants. A facilitator would bring together all delegations particularly interested in the issue under discussion. It is the discretion of the chairperson to choose the facilitator. Of course, acceptance of the person chosen is needed[16] as well as the absence of any opposition to that choice. The choice would be construed either as a reward or as a penalty. It is a reward when the facilitator is chosen because i) s/he[17] has demonstrated understanding of the objections of the delegations not ready to accept a consensus, and ii) s/he possesses the flexibility to look for formulae that might overcome those objections. It is a penalty when the facilitator chosen is perceived as the main stumbling block to obtaining consensus. S/he is then given the opportunity to propose different formulae of meeting their objections without raising new ones. If not successful, s/he would at least be better aware of the difficulties his or her objections cause and of the flexibility needed from him or her toward a positive outcome.

[16] Only once did a proposed facilitator, the head of the delegation of the Holy See, refuse to accept the task The choice was rather a penalty than a reward.

[17] All facilitators were male.

2.1.3 Consensus

Technically speaking, consensus is the adoption of a proposal without a vote. It does not mean that everyone is happy with the result obtained. Those that have serious reservations must be satisfied that it has been possible to alleviate them. Those in favour of the proposal must be satisfied that the essence of the proposal is safeguarded, and that the outcome is preferable to having no result at all. The majority must be willing to accommodate the minority. The minority must be appreciative of the efforts of the majority. The efforts of both the majority and the minority are constantly checked against the criterion of "reasonableness", albeit a relative notion. In exchanging views, arguments are put forward explaining why the proposal should be formulated in one way or another. Those arguments can be of a legal, political, linguistic, historic, or philosophical nature. The better the arguments are developed, the higher the chances of success. If diplomats negotiating human rights documents want to be successful, they must have a solid background in most of those fields. Some delegations from either side may have strong views. Other uncommitted delegations could listen to the merits of the arguments advanced with a more open mind. Once a side succeeds in convincing those other delegations of the reasonableness of its position, they would exercise pressure, first, privately, and later publicly, on the delegations of the other side to give in to the opposite view.

For the WEOG, sticking to consensus was essential.[18] Representing only about 16% of the delegations at the Conference, the chances for that Group winning a vote were minimal. However, after a few days, the Iranian Ambassador Ali Khoram, who chaired the Drafting Committee, proposed to me that, in case I could not obtain a consensus on some paragraphs after having tried several times, I should rule. For me, this was out of the question. Only consensus could lead to success. The next day, he proposed to merge the two Working Groups under his chairpersonship. Ambassador Bonaventure Bowa (Zambia), who chaired the Working Group on the draft Programme of Action, and I were allowed to sit at the right and left sides of Ambassador Khoram respectively. After about an hour, it became obvious that the Working Groups merged into one did not make progress. Giving suit to my desperate appeal to Ambassador Lindgren through eye contact, he took the floor. He stated that there was no improvement compared with the way the two Working Groups functioned separately; the reality was quite the contrary. He proposed to return to the previous setting. His intervention was met by a loud and general applause. In a last attempt, the Iranian Ambassador objected that only one pool of interpreters was available that afternoon. I replied that in the Working Group on the draft Declaration, we had made progress the previous day by working in three languages only, during an evening meeting (from 6 p.m. to 9 p.m.) and even in one language only, during a night meeting (from 9 p.m till 12 p.m). This was the end of the experiment with the

---

[18] Rule 34 of the Rules of Procedure of the Durban Conference states that "The Conference shall exert all possible efforts to ensure that its work and the adoption of its report are accomplished by *general agreement*", but Rule 36 states that "Subject to rule 34, decisions of the Conference on all matters of substance shall be taken by a two thirds majority of representatives present and voting".

merged Working Groups. That "my" Working Group had succeeded the day before to meet without full interpretation made me believe that many delegations that had put much time and energy in discussing the paragraphs of the draft Declaration, would be willing to do the extra effort necessary to go home with a text accepted by consensus.

2.1.4 Rules of Procedure

Knowledge of the rules of procedure was of paramount importance in the last hours of the Conference.[19] The rules of procedure were relegated since the end of the Cold War; participants are less familiar with them. During the Cold War, discussions frequently ended in procedural fights. This was less the case in the subsequent years. Procedural debates often relate to the order of voting.

A crucial factor is the order of submission of proposals. As long as negotiations take place, no proposal is formally submitted. Submitting a proposal signals the end of negotiations. Such an action may have adverse consequences. Opponents may interpret it as an act of bad faith characterized by a lack of flexibility, fairness, and reasonableness. The order of voting could be influenced by submitting amendments, which have priority over proposals. This could give rise to heated discussions to determine whether the modifications proposed are indeed amendments rather than alternative proposals.[20] This could be further complicated by procedural motions concerning the conduct of the meeting.

2.1.5 The "No Action Motion"

A "no action motion" is a very special procedural motion. Voting on such a motion has priority over voting on a proposal. A "no action motion" tends to negate a vote on the substance of the proposal(s) under discussion. Delegations are not very keen to pronounce themselves on the substance of a proposal. This is certainly the case when the proposal criticizes the human rights record of a particular state. In such cases, several delegations are easily inclined to prefer support for such a motion. Voting upon it may be quite popular as it expresses a lack of enthusiasm to be involved in a delicate issue. Subject to pressure to vote one way or another by other states, among them not infrequently very powerful states, delegations may desire to vote in favour of a "no action motion" as a way out of having to take a stand in an embarrassing situation. Particularly, delegations that intend to abstain on the substance of a proposal may easily be seduced into a positive vote on a "no action motion". It is not uncommon that, while there is no majority to reject a proposal,

---

[19] Bossuyt (2001), pp. 12–15, & "Procedural Issues at the Durban Conference against Racism" in *International Human Rights Protection, op. cit.*, pp. 91–101.

[20] Rule 42 states that "A proposal is considered an amendment to another proposal if it merely adds to, deletes from or revises part of that proposal".

there is one in support of a "no action motion" concerning that proposal. That's why "no action motions" are not liked by Western delegations. Quite often, a proposal to condemn a state for human rights violations has not been adopted because a "no action motion" prevented a vote on such a proposal.

A "no action motion" played a decisive role at the end of the World Conference. The Working Group on the draft Declaration held its last meeting on Saturday morning 8 September 2001 from 7 a.m but it had to stop its activities at 10 a.m with only five paragraphs left without consensus. As Chairperson, I drew the conclusion that those paragraphs could not be included in the Declaration. At the Main Committee, the Foreign Minister of Syria, Farouk al-Sharaa, tried a last-minute effort to have three paragraphs included concerning foreign occupation. He considered those paragraphs general in nature and not directed to a specific situation. Other delegations, including those belonging to the WEOG, considered those paragraphs as singling out policies of Israel towards the occupied territories. There was no consensus on the question whether the paragraphs to be adopted on the Middle East would replace those paragraphs. Much to the disappointment of the WEOG, the South African delegation supported the Syrian view at the risk of seeing the Conference collapse in its very last hours.

The Conference was then meeting in the configuration of the Main Committee. Whether they were the two Working Groups, the Drafting Committee, the Main Committee or the Conference itself, all those formats were plenary, but they all had a distinct chair. The Main Committee was chaired by Ambassador Claudio Moreno (Italy). At that Committee, the outcomes of the negotiations on the most sensitive paragraphs concerning the past and the Middle East were presented and adopted. They had been negotiated at the highest level outside the two Working Groups. The Belgian Minister of Foreign Affairs, Louis Michel, presiding over the EU, fulfilled a key role in those negotiations.[21] It is unfortunate that, once the consensus was obtained on those paragraphs, they had not been sent first to the two Working Groups to be inserted in the draft Declaration and in the draft Programme of Action respectively. If that would have been done, several months of controversy and animosity concerning the precise location of those paragraphs in the Declaration and in the Programme of Action could have been avoided.

[21] In her closing statement, Ms Mary Robinson, the United Nations High Commissioner for Human Rights (UNHCHR) said: "Among the delegations it would be invidious to single out individuals, but I feel that I must put on record my appreciation to the Belgian Minister for Foreign Affairs, Louis Michel, who went that extra mile for the Conference" [A/CONF.189/12 (Part III), Annex IV, p. 31]. According to Ambassador Lindgren (*op. cit.*, p. 370, note 13), "Belgium succeeded in keeping the fifteen united and present till the end of the conference, thereby avoiding a block withdrawal that would burry every hope".

2.1.6 The Four Suspensions

After two suspensions of the Main Committee, the very able representative of the UN Legal Counsel had to explain twice that, confronted with text in square brackets (on which there was no consensus), the Main Committee had to take a decision either to delete the square brackets or to delete the text between square brackets. After a third suspension, the Chairperson stated that a vote should be taken. It was ironic that a chairperson belonging to the WEOG proposed to do exactly what the WEOG had consistently opposed. Belgium, on behalf of the EU, requested to avoid a vote at all costs. Brazil stated that it would vote against all paragraphs on which there was no consensus. Canada asked not to go to a vote on those paragraphs. Even the young but extremely active Ms Mumtaz Zahra Baloch of Pakistan agreed that this was not the time for a vote. For the fourth time, Ambassador Moreno adjourned the meeting. This fourth suspension lasted more than two hours.

2.1.7 Submission and Withdrawal of the "No Action Motion"

When the meeting resumed, Ambassador Moreno had left the Conference[22] and was replaced by one of the vice-chairpersons of the Main Committee, Ambassador Alexander Slabý (Czech Republic). He was bound to become permanent representative in Geneva. An appeal by Dr Zuma to conclude was followed by a heated debate.[23] Delegations making more than one intervention were Syria (5), Brazil (5), Pakistan (5), the Russian Federation (3), Algeria (2) and Belgium (2). During that debate, the very experienced Brazilian Ambassador Saboia[24] introduced a "no action motion".[25] While referring to the rule concerning the adjournment of the debate, the (new) chairperson of the Main Committee stated that only two speakers could speak in favour and two against such a motion. New Zealand spoke in favour of the motion. Not without protest, the chairperson of the Main Committee interpreted the statements of Algeria (Ambassador Mohamed-Salah Dembri) and Syria as opposing the motion. This was followed by a highly confused debate in which it was extremely difficult to get the floor. When the chairperson was put under pressure to ask whether Brazil insisted on its motion, Ambassador Saboia withdrew it.

[22] Several delegates encountered difficulties in rescheduling their travel arrangements, since the conference was supposed to finish the day before.

[23] Bossuyt (2016b), pp. 91–102.

[24] At that time, Ambassador Saboia was Secretary of State for Human Rights of Brazil. He had also been, *inter alia*, Chairperson (1996) of the UN Commission on Human Rights.

[25] Rule 44.3 states that "A motion requiring that no decision be taken on a proposal shall be put to the vote before a vote is taken on the proposal in question".

2.1.8 Reintroduction and Voting on the "No Action Motion"

Immediately after the withdrawal of the no action motion, the Russian Federation stated that it had raised its name plate on several occasions to support the Brazilian motion. The Belgian Minister of Justice Marc Verwilghen (at that moment I was sitting next to him)[26] reintroduced the "no action motion" on behalf of the EU.[27] Louis Michel had left the Conference, early in the morning of 8 September 2001, to preside over the informal meeting of the Ministers for Foreign Affairs of EU Member States (Gymnich) in Genval (near Brussels). His arrival in Genval was welcomed by a standing ovation of his colleagues. Louis Michel was originally expected to leave the Conference on 3 September but the US Secretary of State, Colin Powell, announced on that day that the USA had left the Conference. He stated thus: "Today I have instructed our representatives at the World Conference against Racism to return home". That example was immediately followed by the state of Israel, but not by any other state.

While Argentina and the Russian Federation spoke out in favour of the no action motion, Syria and South Africa spoke out against it. The result of the vote (at the request of Australia for a "roll call" vote) was 51 votes[28] to 37[29] with 11 abstentions.[30] The absence or non-participation in the vote of 70 delegations was most astonishing![31] The Syrian Foreign Minister had lost the battle of reasonableness. Once the result was known, it was obvious that further debate was pointless. Soon after, the Conference adopted the Declaration and the Programme of Action without a vote.

3 Conclusion

The UN High Commissioner for Human Rights and Secretary General of the Conference, Mrs Mary Robinson, opened her closing statement, at the Durban Conference, by expressing the views of many in the following words: "It has been an exhausting nine days for all of us, but I believe it has been worth it. We have

---

[26] After the reintroduction of the "no action motion" but before the vote on it, the Belgian Minister of Justice had to leave the conference (see *supra* note 21), he designated me to replace him.

[27] Rule 31, 2nd sentence, states that "A proposal or a motion thus withdrawn may be reintroduced by any representative".

[28] Voted in favour: 23 Western States, 12 Latin-American States, 11 Eastern European States, 3 African States (Gabon, Ghana, and DRC), and 2 Asian States (Fiji and Japan).

[29] Voted against: 19 Asian States, 14 African States and 4 Caribbean States.

[30] Abstained: 4 African States (Kenya, Senegal, Seychelles, and Togo), 3 Asian States (India, Philippines, and Singapore), 3 Eastern European States (Armenia, Azerbaijan, and Bosnia-Hercegovina) and 1 Latin American State (Ecuador).

[31] This was the case of 30 African States, 14 Asian States, 11 Latin American and Caribbean States, 11 Eastern European States and 4 Western States (Andorra, Greece, Iceland, and Malta).

come a very long way. Many questioned whether it would be possible to reach consensus, but we have succeeded and that is no small achievement".[32]

As widely known, three days later on 11 September 2001 ("nine eleven"), two planes flew into the Twin Towers of New York. Strange as it may seem to others, for those who had participated in the Durban World Conference, the surprise was somewhat less.[33] It seems worthwhile to quote the political stocktaking of the Conference made by Pitts:[34]

> The Organization of the Islamic Conference (OIC) and the Palestinians realized their objective of garnering renewed attention and sympathy for the Palestinian cause, at much less cost to the OIC than devoting more direct and substantial resources to helping the Palestinians on the ground. Israel was able to reinforce its status as an underdog state surrounded by hostile states and unsupported by most of the world except its staunch ally the United States of America. The Africans also got attention for their causes and furthered their real agenda of receiving commitments for stepped-up development assistance, investment, and market reforms. The Europeans were able to step in and save the day on the most contentious issues of the conference. The Asians and the Latin Americans played facilitative roles and largely dodged bullets aimed at themselves. The US relished the satisfaction again (recall this was pre-September 11) of acting as tough; it really didn't need the rest of the world.[35]

And finally, I would like to share Pitts' conclusion when he replies to critics of the UN that dismiss conferences such as Durban "as worthless, on grounds that they're merely extraordinarily expensive talking shops that produce mere words that have no real effect combating the world's problems". He opines that "if the UN's value consists largely in providing just such forums for talking (as an alternative to, and safety valve for, more contentious forms of assertion like war), and if words represent ideas which influence life and death in documents ranging from the Bible and Koran to the Communist Manifesto, the Declaration of Independence, and the Universal Declaration of Human Rights, then such conferences have value".[36]

---

[32] Robinson, *op. cit.*, p. 29.

[33] See Pitts, *op. cit.*, p. 22 ("[When I woke up in the morning of September 11], I was struck at once by a strong sense that the two events – Durban and the terrorist attacks - were somehow connected in important basic ways, but in the immediate aftermath the raw horror of September 11 subsumed and obscured these connections. The links to September 11, especially the costs of intolerance, are now becoming clearer") and Lindgren Alves, *op. cit.*, p. 362 ("Because those terrorist acts seemed to bear an irrational relationship with some problems discussed in the meetings, one cannot even deem absurd, though in an evidently wrong, superficial manner, the association of ideas between the suicidal kidnappers of the aircraft transformed into bombs and certain attitudes kept in the discussions").

[34] Pitts, *op. cit.*, p. 22.

[35] Ibid.

[36] Ibid pp. 21–22.

References

Banton M (2002) Lessons from the 2001 World Conference Against Racism. J Ethnic Migr Stud 28(2):355–366

Bossuyt M (2001) Procedural Confusion at the Main Committee of the Durban Conference against Racism. Hum Rights Monit 56:12–15

Bossuyt M (2016a) At the Crossroads of Law and Politics (28 September 2007). In Bossuyt M (ed) International human rights protection: balanced, critical, realistic. Cambridge, Intersentia

Bossuyt M (2016b) Procedural Issues at the World Conference against Racism. In Bossuyt M (ed) International human rights protection: balanced, critical, realistic. Intersentia, pp 91–102

Bossuyt M, Vandeginste S (2001) The issue of reparation for slavery and colonialism and the Durban World Conference against Racism. Hum Rights Law J 31:341–350

Lindgren Alves JA (2003) The Durban Conference against Racism and everyone's responsibilities. Neth Q Hum Rights 21(3):361–384

Pitts C (2001) Anatomy of a World Conference: Was Durban Worthwhile? Hum Rights Monit 56:15–23

Consensus Building and Its Progression in the Durban Process

Catherine S. Namakula

1 Introduction

Despite all the obstacles that had to be overcome, the World Conference against Racism, held from 31 August 2001–08 September 2001 was ultimately successful in negotiating a declaration and programme of action by consensus.[1] The requirement of a simple majority of 51 percent on procedural matters and a two-thirds majority for substantive matters was pursued and met. The Conference had 2300 representatives from 163 countries, including 16 heads of state, 58 foreign ministers, and 44 ministers.[2] The agenda of the Conference was set in the previous year by world leaders that resolved in the Millenium Declaration to take measures to eliminate the increasing acts of racism and xenophobia in many societies and to

[1] See Report of the World Conference against Racism, Racial Discrimination, Xenophobia and Related Intolerance para 20, p. 132. https://www.oas.org/dil/afrodescendants_durban_declaration.pdf. Accessed on 14 June 2025. See also World Conference against Racism, Racial Discrimination, Xenophobia and Related Intolerance: Declaration and Programme of Action, see Introduction.

[2] See Report of the World Conference against Racism, Racial Discrimination, Xenophobia and Related Intolerance, ibid pp. 79–86; Daily Highlights - World Conference against Racism (un.org), https://www.un.org/WCAR/dh/, 08 September 2001.

C. S. Namakula (✉)
University of the Free State, UN Working Group of Experts on People of African Descent, Bloemfontein, South Africa

C. S. Namakula (ed.), *Untold Reflections from the World Conference Against Racism*, SpringerBriefs in Law, https://doi.org/10.1007/978-3-032-17265-5_4

promote greater harmony and tolerance in all societies.[3] The focus of the Durban Conference was action-oriented and practical steps to eradicate racism.[4]

The outcome document followed intensive negotiations of text drawn up with the help of regional groupings including the European Union.[5] The Durban Declaration and Programme of Action (DDPA) is a firm political commitment of the international community to combat racism, racial discrimination, xenophobia and related intolerance. The Conference was preceded by significant preparatory deliberations, including regional conferences in Santiago (Chile), Tehran (Iran), Strabourg (France), Dakar (Senegal), five expert seminars and three sessions of the Preparatory Committee. The Preparatory Committee's mandate was to develop 'the draft agenda, the draft declaration, and the draft programme of action of the World Conference'.[6] It also determined the themes to be included in the provisional agenda for the Conference and established a working group that met between scheduled preparatory committee meetings and the Conference to complete the work that was not finished at formal meetings.[7]

Consensus gathering commenced at the regional level,[8] and considerable time was invested in the process. Mary Robinson, the then UN High Commissioner for Human Rights revealed that lengthy drafting sessions and events of every description had taken place in every part of the world with the focus on the themes of Durban.[9] Work leading to Durban started as early as the first World Conference to Combat Racism and Racial Discrimination in 1978—the midpoint of the decade on racism, followed by the second World Conference to Combat Racism and Racial Discrimination in 1983; there was no novelty at the Durban Conference. Advocate Mojankunyane Gumbi, a key negotiator of the Durban Declaration and Programme

[3] Report of the World Conference against Racism, Racial Discrimination, Xenophobia and Related Intolerance, ibid p. 149. United Nations Millenium Declaration, General Assembly Resolution 55/2, 08 September 2000, para 25. https://www.ohchr.org/en/instruments-mechanisms/instruments/united-nations-millennium-declaration. Accessed 14 June 2025.

[4] Contribution to the World Conference against Racism, Racial Discrimination, Xenophobia and Related Intolerance I EUR-Lex (europa.eu). https://eur-lex.europa.eu/EN/legal-content/summary/contribution-to-the-world-conference-against-racism-racial-discrimination-xenophobia-and-related-intolerance.html. Accessed 14 June 2025.

[5] Ibid.

[6] See Report of the Preparatory Committee on its First Session, U.N. GAOR, Hum. Rts. Comm., 1st Sess., U.N. Doc. A/CONF.189/PC.1/21 (2000), available *at* http://www.unhchr.ch/huridocda/huridoca.nsf/ (Symbol) /A.CONF. I 89.PC. 1.21 .En?Opendocument [hereinafter *First PrepCom].*

[7] Ibid.

[8] For example, at the regional meeting of the Americas, 'the representatives of the participating countries of Latin America and the Caribbean, the United States and Canada reached important agreements on the issues involved and these agreements delivered a basic consensus effectively capable of global projection'. https://www.un.org/WCAR/statements/chilE.htm.

[9] Statement by Mrs. Mary Robinson, United Nations High Commissioner for Human Rights and Secretary-General of the World Conference against Racism, Racial Discrimination, Xenophobia and Related Intolerance, p. 159. Available at: https://www.oas.org/dil/afrodescendants_durban_declaration.pdf.

of Action,[10] noted that 'Durban was a continuation; nothing was said or done in Durban that had not been done before in the many fora of the UN. There was nothing in the DDPA that had not been discussed including the difficult matters such as the right to self-determination, the conflict between Israel and Palestine, and reparations, and yet the negotiations evolved the way they did'.

It was however demonstrably clear from the early stages that certain issues posed considerable difficulty including Palestine/Middle East, slavery and colonialism, compensation and reparations, migration, refugees, internally displaced persons and xenophobia, trafficking in women and children, indigenous people and religious intolerance (specifically Islamaphobia and Zionism).[11] In slavery, the world was confronting a very difficult question by itself and its legacies, requiring taking huge obligations and making radical changes to law, policy, and practice. This chapter includes perspectives of the legends of Durban on the views attempting to reverse the Durban Declaration and Programme of Action. Voices contesting the Durban consensus raise key questions such as the legitimacy of the Durban consensus and whether concluded and documented consensus could be retrospectively challenged or withdrawn. It is intended to trace the origins, evolution, and acquisition of the Durban consensus, through the experiences, and undertakings of the legends and luminaries of the World Conference against Racism.

2 South Africa's Leadership

Mrs. Mary Robinson described South Africa as the moral leader of the world against racism.[12] South Africa itself considered it a moral responsibility to host the World Conference against racism four years after obtaining its independence. It was persuaded to do so on the premise that South Africa, having overcome racism in a particular form, could set an example for the world about the importance of fighting it. 'It was hard to think of anywhere else where the struggle against racism and discrimination [had] been most significant. The nation symbolized the struggle against racism'.[13] The world drew inspiration from the heroic victory of the people of South

[10] Currently Special advisor to the Secretary General of the UN on addressing racism in the workplace (from 2023-), and formerly Special Advisor to former President Thabo Mbeki (1999–2008).

[11] See Foreign Affairs Portfolio Committee on the World Conference Against Racism: Briefing by Department I PMG, 28 March 2001. https://pmg.org.za/committee-meeting/419/. Accessed 14 June 2025.

[12] Plenary meeting of the World Conference Statement by Mary Robinson, High Commissioner for Human Rights and Secretary-General of the World Conference against Racism, Racial Discrimination, Xenophobia and Related Intolerance I OHCHR. https://www.ohchr.org/en/statements-and-speeches/2009/10/plenary-meeting-world-conference-statement-mary-robinson-high.

[13] Statement by Chilean Minister of Planning and Cooperation_ Mrs Alejandra Krauss, World Conference against Racism, Racial Discrimination, Xenophobia and other related Intolerances. <https://www.un.org/WCAR/statements/chilE.htm>. Accessed 13 June 2025. See also statement by Kofi Annan, then Secretary General of the United Nations 'Where else, my friends, could we

Africa against the institutionalized system of apartheid, as well as for equality and justice.[14] South Africa embraced the role of facilitating consensus on even the contentious issues for the outcome to be adhered to and implemented by all member states.[15]

Durban demanded much and the luminaries gave it all. Mrs. Mary Robinson described the experience as an exhausting nine days for all of them.[16] President Thabo Mbeki lost his father during the Conference but could not leave the deliberations until the final moments leading to his father's burial. South Africa's Foreign Minister Dr Zuma spent hours of day and night, during and preceding the Conference, negotiating the agreed consensus positions, which were achieved. The Conference went on for one more day than the days stipulated by the UN. UN officials were prepared to work an extra day, without pay, to assist the Chairperson in advancing the results. Dr Dlamini and President Mbeki went to great length in ensuring that there was nothing in the language of the document that would be subject to valid criticism.

Durban gave the world a moment to pose and reflect and recommit itself to the fundamental truth that all people are born free and equal in dignity.[17] Nothing that led to Durban prepared the participants for what Durban would become.[18] There was manifestation of what was described as manufactured rage at the forum of Non-Governmental Organisations (NGOs), which sadly had no clear basis. The subsequent government negotiations commenced in a difficult environment set by the proceedings at the NGO forum. The NGO Forum took place from 28 August to 1 September 2001.[19] It was the conclusion of a process that began at the Strasbourg preparatory conference in October 2000 and was attended by 8000 individuals

---

hold this Conference? Who could teach us how to overcome racism, discrimination and intolerance, if not the people of this country?' See Report of the World Conference against Racism, Racial Discrimination, Xenophobia and Related Intolerance, p. 146. Accessed from https://www.oas.org/dil/afrodescendants_durban_declaration.pdf.

[14] See Report of the World Conference against Racism, Racial Discrimination, Xenophobia and Related Intolerance. Durban, 31 August–08 September 2001, note 2 above.

[15] See Foreign Affairs Portfolio Committee on the World Conference Against Racism: Briefing by Department | PMG, note 12 above. Available at: https://pmg.org.za/committee-meeting/419/.

[16] Statement by Mrs. Mary Robinson, United Nations High Commissioner for Human Rights and Secretary-General of the World Conference against Racism, Racial Discrimination, Xenophobia and Related Intolerance, Annexed to the Report of the World Conference against Racism, Racial Discrimination, Xenophobia and Related Intolerance. Durban, 31 August–08 September 2001, note 2 above, p. 174.

[17] Advocate Mojankunyane Gumbi, Address during Memoirs of Durban, an event during the public session of the Working Group of experts on people of African descent, May 2023, Geneva, Switzerland.

[18] Ibid.

[19] NGO Forum Declaration for the World Conference against Racism, Racial Discrimination, Xenophobia and other forms of Intolerance, 03 September 2001. https://www.hurights.or.jp/wcar/E/ngofinaldc.htm. Accessed 14 June 2025.

representing close to 3000 NGOs from all continents.[20] For five days, NGOs discussed issues of racism, racial discrimination, xenophobia and related intolerance, and shared their own experiences. Twenty-five thematic commissions were created and the results of these were submitted to the Drafting Committee for the NGO Declaration and Plan of Action. The Conference itself had nearly 4000 representatives of NGOs,[21] but it did not take formal note of all parallel activities including the NGO Forum.[22] This was a sign of the Conference's disassociation from the mishaps of the forum.

Ambassador Abdul Minty recalls that on the eve of the Conference, when other organisations and institutions legitimately debated other related issues in their own context, certain persons tried to overflow those issues to the organisers of the Conference and other supporters, which affected the credibility of the Conference in a certain way. There were presumptions that the discussions of the NGOs regarded as setting the tone would be the outcomes of the Conference and needed not be supported. There were various efforts to dissuade governments from attending the Conference. Subsequently Israel and the United States withdrew from the conference but later affirmed the physical presence of their designated representatives, so they had not formally withdrawn. According to Ambassador Minty, 'this was double talk in a situation where they wanted to satisfy certain forces to show their opposition to the Conference and to others the legitimacy of the Conference'.[23] For Israel and the US, no matter what language was used to create compromises and acceptable positions; the outcome would not be acceptable to them. It was a predetermined position to reject the DDPA before it existed. They did not want to move forward in the manner the world had found an opportunity to do so according to Ambassador Minty.

Koffi Annan, former UN Secretary General, while closing the Conference regretted that 'the useful work of the Conference was overshadowed by disagreements on one or two highly controversial emotional issues especially the Middle East. Many hateful things were said particularly in the draft document submitted by the NGO Forum (with emphasis), which tended to inflame the atmosphere rather than encourage rational and constructive discussion'.[24] It was considered essential to deal with all matters of racism hence the perseverance in dealing with the paragraphs on the

[20] See Report of the World Conference against Racism, Racial Discrimination, Xenophobia and Related Intolerance. Durban, 31 August–08 September 2001, note 2 above, p. 177.

[21] Daily Highlights - World Conference against Racism (un.org), 08 September 2001. https://www.un.org/WCAR/dh/.

[22] See Report of the World Conference against Racism, Racial Discrimination, Xenophobia and Related Intolerance. Durban, 31 August–08 September 2001. A/CONF.189/2, note 2 above, p. 179.

[23] Address of Amb Minty at a Special event titled 'Memoirs of Durban by the legends of Durban' during the 32nd public session of the UN Working Group of experts on people of African descent, Geneva, Switzerland.

[24] Statement by Secretary-General on Conclusion of World Conference Against Racism, Racial Discrimination, Xenophobia and Related Intolerance, 08 September 2001. https://press.un.org/en/2001/sgsm7944.doc.htm. Accessed 14 June 2025.

Middle East, however contentious they seemed.[25] Koffi Annan continued that 'the UN is a mirror to the world and its work reflects what divides us as well as what unites us. This can be painful, but it is sometimes necessary. Since it is only if we see our divisions clearly can we work to overcome them'.

3 The Regional Meetings: The Roadmap to Durban

The Office of the High Commissioner for Human Rights facilitated regional meetings of governments and Non-Governmental Organisations in preparation for the Third World Conference against Racism. Each region raised priority sub-themes in the declarations made. Mrs Mary Robinson noted that the recommendations adopted by the various preparatory meetings showed a high degree of consensus.[26] She noted that 'our journey to Durban has helped to shape thinking about who the victims of racism and discrimination are, what sort of remedies can be made available and the best kinds of preventive measures…the greater understanding which has been achieved of the sources, causes of and remedies for racism must weigh heavily in its favour'.[27]

The European Conference titled 'All different, all equal: from principle to practice' met between 11–13 October 2000 in Strasbourg, France, the Headquarters of the Council of Europe. This was Europe's regional contribution to the World Conference against Racism, Racial Discrimination, Xenophobia and Related Intolerance.[28] It convened 41 member states from the Council of Europe and its bodies, states with observer status to the Council of Europe, governments belonging to the Western Europe and Others Group (WEOG) and the Eastern European Group. The European Conference called for acknowledgment of the suffering caused by slavery and colonialism[29] in contrast to the urge for reparations, expressed by other regional meetings. It was however emphatic about legal protection measures including implementation of relevant international legal instruments, comprehensive anti-discrimination legislation at the national level,[30] adequate reparation of damage

[25] Mr. Ali Khorram, Chairperson of the Drafting Committee, Press Briefing by Chairman of Drafting Committee, 06 September 2001. https://www.un.org/WCAR/pressreleases/khorrambrf.htm. Accessed 13 June 2025.

[26] See summary of report on regional meetings. Accessed from https://www.unic.un.org.pl/durban/regional1.pdf, at p. 12. Accessed 14 June 2025.

[27] Statement by Mrs. Mary Robinson, United Nations High Commissioner for Human Rights and Secretary-General of the World Conference against Racism, Racial Discrimination, Xenophobia and Related Intolerance, pp. 160–161. Accessed from https://www.oas.org/dil/afrodescendants_durban_declaration.pdf.

[28] General Conclusions of the European Conference against Racism, 16 October 2000. https://tandis.odihr.pl/explore?bitstream_id=22317&handle=20.500.12389/19346&provider=iiif-image#?c=0&m=0&s=0&cv=1&xywh=2180%2C144%2C2939%2C1360. Accessed 14 June 2025.

[29] Ibid p. 3.

[30] Ibid para 8.

suffered as a result of discrimination,[31] comprehensive national strategies against racism in policies,[32] integrating a gender perspective,[33] among other practices.

The Asian Regional Preparatory Meeting for the World Conference against Racism, Racial Discrimination, Xenophobia and Related Intolerance was held in Tehran between 19-21 February 2001.[34] Attended by 40 member states from the region, it was preceded by a meeting of 150 Non-Governmental Organisations from 17 to 18 February 2001. The declaration of the Asian Preparatory Meeting contains bold pronouncements about sources, causes, forms and contemporary manifestations of racism; the victims of racism; prevention strategies especially education as the key to promoting respect for racial, ethnic, cultural and linguistic diversity of societies; and remedies including reparation.[35] The matters and persons of concern for the Asian region included the intersectionality of gender and racism; caste and racism; indigenous people and racism; national minorities and racism; people under foreign occupation, refugees and internally displaced persons; migrants and trafficked persons and racism.[36]

The Africa regional preparatory meeting for the World Conference against Racism, Racial Discrimination, Xenophobia and Related Intolerance was a three-day event held in Dakar, Senegal in January 2001. The meeting was attended by 40 government delegations, Non-Governmental Organisations and observers from other regional groups. Recommendations relating to reparations for slave trade, colonialism and apartheid were prioritized. It was decided that slavery is a crime against humanity that needed to be compensated.[37] The meeting recommended to the World Conference i) the establishment of a follow up mechanism entrusted with the supervision of the implementation of the Declaration and Programme of Action to be adopted by the World Conference; ii) the establishment of an international compensation scheme for victims of the slave trade and victims of transnational racist policies and acts; iii) establishment of a development reparation fund for the development process in countries affected by colonialism; iv) to define the modalities of reparation and compensation in a practical and result oriented manner.[38]

---

[31] Ibid para 9.

[32] Ibid para 16.

[33] Ibid para 17.

[34] See Regional Meeting on Anti-Racism, FOCUS, March 2001, Vol. 23. https://www.hurights.or.jp/archives/focus/section2/2001/03/regional-meeting-on-anti-racism.html. Accessed 14 June 2025.

[35] See Declaration of the Asian Preparatory Meeting for the World Conference against Racism, Racial Discrimination, Xenophobia, and Related Intolerance, WCR/RCONF/TEHRAN/2001/L.1/Rev.1, 21 February 2001. Available from: https://www.hurights.or.jp/wcar/E/tehran/intergovdec.htm.

[36] See Declaration of the Asia Pacific NGO Forum, Asia-Pacific NGO Movement for WCAR, Tehran, Iran, February 17–18, 2001. https://www.hurights.or.jp/wcar/E/tehran/ngostatement.htm.

[37] See Foreign Affairs Portfolio Committee, World Conference against Racism, 28 March 2001, note 12 above.

[38] Report of the Regional Conference for Africa [in preparation for the World Conference against Racism, Racial Discrimination, Xenophobia and Related Intolerance], Dakar, 22–24 January 2001, paras 1–4. https://digitallibrary.un.org/record/439789?ln=ar&v=pdf.

4 Structures for Dialogue at the World Conference Against Racism

At the first plenary meeting on 31 August 2001, the Conference established the Main Committee, a Credentials Committee,[39] the Drafting Committee and the two working groups of the Drafting Committee: the working group on the Draft Declaration and the working group on the Draft Programme of Action.[40] These entities were supported by regional groups, and 50 informal consultation groups, which were dismantled upon completing their work of negotiating the difficult issues or ones where consensus could not easily be found.[41] The mere consideration of these issues made some to expect to account—this was the underlying complexity of Durban. Following consultations, the President of the Conference introduced several paragraphs to the Main Committee, which were considered, approved and incorporated in the draft declaration and draft programme of action.[42] In her words 'At each point along the way, we had to respond creatively to both anticipated and unanticipated events'.[43] The Main Committee forwarded the draft declaration and draft programme of action for consideration by the last plenary meeting of the Conference on 08 September 2001.

4.1 *Drafting Committee*

The Drafting Committee decided that the draft declaration and the draft programme of action would be considered by two working groups of the Drafting Committee.[44] By 06 September 2001, Working Group I of the Drafting Committee still had 63

---

[39] To consider the Credentials of representatives of states—see Report of the World Conference against Racism, Racial Discrimination, Xenophobia and Related Intolerance. Durban, 31 August–08 September 2001, note 2 above, p. 115.

[40] Report of the Main Committee para 19, p. 90, annexed to the Report of the World Conference against Racism, Racial Discrimination, Xenophobia and Related Intolerance. Durban, 31 August–08 September 2001, ibid.

[41] Press Briefing by Chairman of Drafting Committee, 06 September 2001, note 25 above. https://www.un.org/WCAR/pressreleases/khorrambrf.htm.

[42] Report of the World Conference against Racism, Racial Discrimination, Xenophobia and Related Intolerance. Durban, 31 August–08 September 2001, note 2 above, pp. 104–106.

[43] Statement by H.E. Ms. Nkosazana Dlamini Zuma, Minister for Foreign Affairs of the Republic of South Africa and President of the World Conference against Racism, Racial Discrimination, Xenophobia and Related Intolerance. Annexed to the Report of the World Conference against Racism, Racial Discrimination, Xenophobia and Related Intolerance. Durban, 31 August–08 September 2001, ibid, p. 172.

[44] See Report of the Main Committee para 7, p. 103, annexed to the Report of the World Conference against Racism, Racial Discrimination, Xenophobia and Related Intolerance. Durban, 31 August–08 September 2001, ibid.

paragraphs of the draft declaration to adopt before the intended end of the Conference the following day; 33 paragraphs related to the so-called 'difficult issues'.[45] 'Working Group II on the draft programme of action had adopted 180 paragraphs, leaving 80 outstanding. Of those, 40 to 45 were being negotiated in the four informal consultation groups dealing with the 'difficult issues' especially the Middle East question, issues relating to the legacy of the past, the grounds of racism, and the categorization of victims of racism.[46] There were more than 50 informal consultation groups negotiating the difficult issues besides the two working groups and the four informal groups.[47] The group facilitating negotiations on the Middle East was dealing with 25–30 paragraphs, the group facilitating negotiations on the past was handling approximately 70 paragraphs.[48]

4.2 *The Main Committee*

Following its establishment at the first plenary of the Conference, the Main Committee held three meetings on 02, 07 and 08 September 2001.[49] Among the key documents transmitted by the Secretary-General of the Conference to the Main Committee for consideration were the draft Declaration of the World Conference and the draft Programme of Action of the World Conference.[50]

At the third meeting of 08 September 2001 (the last and extra day of the Conference), the Main Committee decided to adopt the paragraphs or parts of paragraphs that had been adopted by the two working groups and the Drafting Committee, to delete those paragraphs or parts of paragraphs that had not been adopted by the two working groups and the Drafting Committee and to transmit the amended texts of the draft Declaration and the draft Programme of Action to the plenary of the Conference for consideration.[51]

The Main Committee held a procedural discussion with regard to the paragraphs on which consensus had not been reached in the Drafting Committee.[52] Statements were made by representatives of Armenia, Belgium (on behalf of the European Union), Bosnia and Herzegovina, Canada, Egypt, India, Iran (Islamic Republic of), Kenya, Lebanon, Mexico, Pakistan, the Philippines, the Russian Federation,

[45] Press Briefing by Chairman of Drafting Committee, 06 September 2001, note 25 above. https://www.un.org/WCAR/pressreleases/khorrambrf.htm.

[46] Ibid.

[47] Ibid.

[48] Ibid.

[49] Report of the Main Committee para 3, p. 103, annexed to the Report of the World Conference against Racism, Racial Discrimination, Xenophobia and Related Intolerance. Durban, 31 August–08 September 2001, note 2 above.

[50] Ibid para 4, p. 103.

[51] See Report of the Main Committee ibid para 21, p. 111.

[52] See Report of the Main Committee ibid para 12, p. 110.

Singapore, Spain, the Syrian Arab Republic, Turkey and the United Arab Emirates.[53] On 08 September 2001, the Main Committee considered the draft Declaration and Programme of Action agreed upon in the two working groups and in the drafting committee, submitted by the chairperson of the drafting committee.[54]

The Main Committee decided to take a roll call vote on a motion originally made by Brazil, and reintroduced by Belgium that no action is taken on the paragraphs that had not been considered or had not been adopted by the working groups based on 51 votes to 37 with 11 abstentions.[55]

5 The Position of the United States: The Lehtinen Prophesy

Preceding Durban, the U.S Congress Sub-Committee on International Operations and Human Rights met on Tuesday 31 July 2001 to discuss the nation's position leading up to the Durban World Conference against Racism. The US position was described as forward looking or not looking backwards at all.[56] This resolve aligned with the aspiration of the General Affairs Council of the European Union that the Action Programme and Declaration are forward looking and oriented towards action.[57] Ros-Lehtinen noted that the legitimacy and effectiveness of the World Conference against Racism was majorly threatened by the hostile anti-Semitic, anti-Israel language shepherded by Iran, Iraq and Syria, among other countries and similar provisions that permeated throughout the document.[58] This risk was mitigated by representatives of major sectors of the NGO community and the High Commissioner denouncing the anti-Semitic speech and activities.[59] 'INGOs objected to the language of the NGO text presented to the Third Preparatory Committee Meeting in July in Geneva'. McDougall distinguishes between a discourse that is critical of the Israeli government policy and the articulation of views that are anti-Semitic.[60] Iran lamented that 'all efforts made by the members of the Organization of the Islamic Conference to justly address the causes of the oppressed Palestinian people were

[53] Report of the Main Committee ibid para 12, p. 110.

[54] Report of the Main Committee ibid para 9, p. 110.

[55] Report of the Main Committee ibid paras 17–19, pp. 110–111.

[56] A Discussion on the U.N. World Conference Against Racism (house.gov), hearing before the subcommittee on International Operations and Human Rights of the Committee on International Relations House of Representatives, 107th Congress, First Session, 31 July 2001, p. 171. https://commdocs.house.gov/committees/intlrel/hfa74408.000/hfa74408_0f.htm.

[57] Council Conclusions on the World Conference against Racism, Racial Discrimination, Xenophobia and Related Intolerance. General Affairs Council - 16 July 2001. https://eur-lex.europa.eu/EN/legal-content/summary/contribution-to-the-world-conference-against-racism-racial-discrimination-xenophobia-and-related-intolerance.html.

[58] Ibid pp. 13, 18.

[59] McDougall (2002), p. 146.

[60] Ibid at p. 142.

rendered futile in the atmosphere of intimidation, threat and ultimatum'.[61] Advocate Gumbi recalls that all contentious language was removed from the document. This position is substantiated by Iran's complaint that 'all the paragraphs on the Middle East and Palestinian issue were deleted and were subsequently replaced by new paragraphs in the final documents, despite opposition of the respective parties concerned'.[62] Iran consequently disassociated itself from all paragraphs pertaining to the Palestinian and Middle East issue as falling short of addressing the fundamental issues of the situation in the Middle East, and lacking in fairness, balance and credibility.[63] It is important to note that Iran only withdrew from specific paragraphs of the Durban Declaration and Programme of Action and that it was at liberty to make such reservations and make a bold public statement of its position, which is included in the report of the Conference, despite claims of intimidation. The President of the Conference described Durban as a truly inclusive and broadly consultative process.[64] Other countries that made reservations to (certain) paragraphs that related to the Middle East and the past included Barbados, Guatemala, Iraq, the United Arab Emirates, Bahrain, Kuwait, Oman, Qatar and Saudi Arabia, among others. The Syrian Arab Republic, also singled out by Ros-Lehtinen confirmed joining the draft Declaration other than the Islamic paper without hesitation, to consolidate South Africa's legitimate leadership and reinforce global solidarity and the success of the Conference.[65] Countries that unequivocally joined the consensus and made statements to that effect include Brazil, Japan, and Venezuela, among others.

Ros-Lehtinen highlighted some provisions of the draft Programme of Action that supposedly infringed upon the sovereignty of participating nations such as paragraph New 170, which 'urge(d) all States to refrain from taking any measure leading to the recognition of Jerusalem as the capital of Israel'. This wording is not part of the final document. She suggested replacing words such as 'affirms', 'urges', and 'should' with phrases calling on countries to 'consider adopting appropriate measures' to obtain broad support other than failure of paragraphs.[66] It is not clear why such feeble language that revises and reduces commitment was expected of the DDPA in contrast to the firm language in the earlier proclaimed Beijing Declaration

[61] See Report of the World Conference against Racism, Racial Discrimination, Xenophobia and Related Intolerance. Durban, 31 August–08 September 2001, note 2 above, p. 125.

[62] Ibid.

[63] Ibid.

[64] See Statement by H.E. Ms. Nkosazana Dlamini Zuma, Minister for Foreign Affairs of the Republic of South Africa and President of the World Conference against Racism, Racial Discrimination, Xenophobia and Related Intolerance. Report of the World Conference against Racism, Racial Discrimination, Xenophobia and Related Intolerance. Durban, 31 August–08 September 2001, ibid, p. 173.

[65] Report of the World Conference against Racism, Racial Discrimination, Xenophobia and Related Intolerance. Durban, 31 August–08 September 2001, ibid p. 127.

[66] Council Conclusions on the World Conference against Racism, Racial Discrimination, Xenophobia and Related Intolerance. General Affairs Council - 16 July 2001, p. 11. Available from: https://eur-lex.europa.eu/EN/legal-content/summary/contribution-to-the-world-conference-against-racism-racial-discrimination-xenophobia-and-related-intolerance.html.

and Platform of Action, which 'urges'[67] and even 'strongly urges'[68] states and other stakeholders to take action, with generous use of the 'should' and even 'must' in its text.[69] Ros-Lehtinen also alluded to the controversy that surrounded the issue of reparations especially their scope and time parameters, a key concern that South Africa (the host) expected to decrease the level of participation in the Conference.[70] She juxtaposed the paragraph that called for 'prompt, adequate, and fair reparations and compensation' for victims of slavery, regardless of when the abuse or violations were committed, with one calling for the establishment of more effective, preventive and deterrent measures to provide adequate compensation of victims of racial discrimination including by means of truth commissions, apologies and the establishment of victims' compensation and reparation funds as forward looking.[71] She therefore advocated for a position that gave persons making reparations more discretion over the processes than the affected persons on their own reparation. The claims for reparations are often channeled into a discourse of development cooperation,[72] which is often conditional and of doubtful impact. The profile of the victims' views on reparation have since been centralized in the description of reparation in international law.[73] Following consultations, the President of the Conference, in the final days of the Conference, intervened to harmonise language on specific matters such as legacies of the past and introduced new paragraphs to the draft outcome document.[74] This was a tactical move that set the conference outcomes on a positive trajectory.

Ms. Ros-Lehtinen intimated that provisions of the Durban Declaration and Programme of Action that extended future compensation to States, communities and individuals that were victims of policies based on national superiority, colonial or other forms of alien domination or foreign occupation were of such broad application that could have a destabilizing effect worldwide.[75] The 'Western Europe and

[67] Beijing Declaration and Programme of Action para 87 (a), 106 (k). Available from: https://www.unwomen.org/sites/default/files/Headquarters/Attachments/Sections/CSW/PFA_E_Final_WEB.pdf.

[68] Ibid para 38.

[69] Ibid Foreword, para 9, 29, 36, 40, 47, 94, 106, 123.

[70] See Foreign Affairs Portfolio Committee, World Conference against Racism, 28 March 2001. World Conference Against Racism: Briefing by Department | PMG. https://pmg.org.za/committee-meeting/419/. Accessed 13 June 2025.

[71] A Discussion on the U.N. World Conference Against Racism (house.gov), p. 12. Available from: https://commdocs.house.gov/committees/intlrel/hfa74408.000/hfa74408_0f.htm.

[72] See McDougall (2002) note 59 above, at p. 139.

[73] Situation in the Democratic Republic of Congo in the case of the Prosecutor v Thomas Lubanga Dyilo, Decision establishing the principles and procedures to be applied to reparations, ICC-01/04-01/06, 07 August 2012, para 31: realistic needs and expectations of victims have to be taken in to account. Available from: https://www.icc-cpi.int/sites/default/files/CourtRecords/CR2012_07872.PDF.

[74] Para 10, p. 104.

[75] A Discussion on the U.N. World Conference Against Racism (house.gov), p. 13. Available from: https://commdocs.house.gov/committees/intlrel/hfa74408.000/hfa74408_0f.htm.

Others Group' (WEOG) including the European Union, the United States, Canada, Australia, New Zealand and Japan strenuously opposed the language that guaranteed compensation or reparation in the DDPA.[76] Little wonder the voices of dissent against Durban are escalating as the call for reparations becomes bolder within the framework of the programme of activities for the International Decade of People of African descent. It is arguable that the failure to address this question has kept the parts of the World that are under foreign systems of domination unstable with recent outbursts in West Africa, and unrest in the Chagos Islands, among other jurisdictions. There are clear compensation disparities based on the identity of the beneficiaries; for example, in 2022, Sudan paid $335 million as retroactive punitive damages to the United States for the bombings of the US Embassies in Kenya and Tanzania, by al-Qaeda in 1998. This followed a US Supreme Court decision affirming a retrospective law of Congress and an allegation that Sudan had provided shelter and other material support to al-Qaeda,[77] an allegation that Sudan denies. Haiti has paid millions of dollars as indemnity to French plantation owners for property, including enslaved persons, lost in the revolution that won Haiti's independence in 1804.[78]

Mr. Wareham of the December 12th Movement addressed the U.S Congress Sub-Committee on International Operations and Human Rights about the obstructionist tactics employed by the U.S, the very reason why there was no agreed upon draft four weeks to the Conference. His organization had organized around the World Conference against Racism from its inception and had participated in the preparatory meetings in Geneva, Santiago, Adisa Ababa, Atlanta, Chicago, Johannesburg, Honduras, and Washington D.C. Mr. Wareham contended that the decisions and actions of the U.S had to be assessed against the background of the reality in the country. He traced racism to the foundations of the United States as illustrated in the country's first Constitution; he also referred to the assertion in the Kerner Commission report that the U.S was 'two societies, one black, one white, separate and unequal'.[79] Of note, the United States together with Israel withdrew from the World Conference against Racism.[80]

The US also withdrew from the Durban Review Conference of 2009 opposing the reaffirmation of the Durban Declaration and Programme of Action (DDPA) in

[76] See Camponovo (2003), p. 670.

[77] Opati v Republic of Sudan No. 17-1268; Sudan Claims Resolution Act, Dec. 2022. Accessed from https://www.gao.gov/assets/gao-23-105782.pdf.

[78] Oosterlinck et al. (2022), p. 1249.

[79] A Discussion on the U.N. World Conference Against Racism (house.gov), p. 191. Available from: https://commdocs.house.gov/committees/intlrel/hfa74408.000/hfa74408_0f.htm.

[80] See Plenary meeting of the World Conference Statement by Mary Robinson, High Commissioner for Human Rights and Secretary-General of the World Conference against Racism, Racial Discrimination, Xenophobia and Related Intolerance | OHCHR. https://www.ohchr.org/en/statements-and-speeches/2009/10/plenary-meeting-world-conference-statement-mary-robinson-high. Accessed 13 June 2025.

the text of the review conference.[81] Durban opponents are not sparing efforts to disrupt any logical efforts to enhance further deliberations on implementing the commitments under the DDPA. Diana Ralph of Independent Jewish Voices described her experience of the 2009 review conference as follows:

> There were 1400 or so Israel lobby observers who came in, with their way paid by the World Jewish Congress and by a variety of others, such as the Simon Wiesenthal Centre, and other organizations; those were two of the main ones. They came in equipped with information about which UN delegates they were to lobby and harass, and what they were going to do when Ahmadinejad came to speak. Any head of state is allowed to speak to address any UN conference like that. So, as it turned out, there had been this smear campaign against the World Conference against Racism, so that no other head of state had asked to speak. The only head of state who asked to speak was Ahmadinejad.[82]

6 Conclusion

Brazil was emphatic that 'political questions and undertones should by no means tarnish our achievements in Durban'.[83] The footprint of the World Conference against Racism comprises of significant milestones including obtaining consensus over such complex matters. In his opening remarks, former President Thabo Mbeki expressed his expectation of the World Conference to indicate what is to be done practically so that the call to end despair and human degradation in all countries results in a changed and changing world in which all human beings actually enjoy the inalienable right to human dignity.[84] Durban was decisively consensual; it produced a plan of action that is instructive and obliging. What needs to be done is to give effect to the decisions taken at Durban.

Ambassador Abdul Minty recalls that the question they had to ask after the Conference in Durban was whether the world was ready to fight racism and they noticed that the world was not ready to do so. The nature of the DDPA as an action oriented and practical document against a phenomenon that some were unprepared to confront could potentially lead to resentment. The US has seemingly remained under the weight of the Lehtinen prophesy of doom, despite being overtaken by events and used its influence to mislead a few unsuspecting allies. This surprised

[81] Pillay shocked by US withdrawal from Durban Review Conference | OHCHR, Press Releases, Office of the High Commissioner for Human Rights, 19 April 2009. https://www.ohchr.org/en/press-releases/2009/10/pillay-shocked-us-withdrawal-durban-review-conference. Accessed 14 June 2025.

[82] Interview by Abigail B. Bakan on 04 March 2012 reflected in Bakan and Bakan (2017), p. 229.

[83] See Report of the World Conference against Racism, Racial Discrimination, Xenophobia and Related Intolerance. Durban, 31 August–08 September 2001, note 2 above, p. 133.

[84] Address of the President of South Africa, Thabo Mbeki, at the Opening of the World Conference Against Racism, Racial Discrimination, Xenophobia and Related Intolerance, Durban, 31 August 2001 | OHCHR. https://www.ohchr.org/en/statements-and-speeches/2009/10/address-president-south-africa-thabo-mbeki-opening-world-conference. Accessed 15 June 2025.

persons such as Mary Robinson, who reckons that perhaps the September 11, 2001 attacks on the United States prevented the proper assessment of the importance of the Durban Declaration and Programme of Action.[85] The anti-Semitic comments that arose during the NGO Conference were 'challenged and resoundingly renounced' and a clear consensus emerged.[86] If it were not so, many more countries other than the US and Israel would have withdrawn from Durban in Durban because anti-Semitism is a concern for all humanity. Ambassador Minty underscores the significance of remembering that there is nothing in the Durban Declaration and Programme of Action that is anti-Semitic. There is no racism in reverse in any of its specifications.

The other question for consideration is whether the controversies that characterized consensus building towards Durban fundamentally eroded the integrity of the Durban Declaration and Programme of Action. The unfavourable atmosphere created by the US and Israel campaign would have consumed the DDPA by now if it did not have the credibility and value it has. The US campaign against Durban characterizes reading the complexities that were navigated during consensus building over thorny global issues into a written consensus document, with the effect of placing the victims of racism and other forms of intolerance to strict proof of how the framework that was intended to support them was not victimizing anybody else. It is relying on the inevitable contentious matters that arose during the negotiations and were effectively addressed by the process to discredit the outcome, hence walking back on its commitment to be forward looking. The United States is still holding on to a prophesy that was overtaken by the skillful actions of the leadership of the World Conference and the resolve of the global community to confront the evil of racism, which emerged stronger than divergency of opinions. The advancement of this regressive and indefensible agenda must be rejected at all costs. The World must continue to refuse to accept to make a statement, as it did at Durban, that the human rights of some are superior to the human rights of others.[87] President Thabo Mbeki rightly foretold that those that benefit from the silence and invisibility of those who suffer from racism, racial discrimination, xenophobia and related intolerance would continue to argue that affected persons are wrong to represent their cause, that they are mistaken to broadcast the pain they feel, as they attempted to do so at Durban. That they would ask them to talk about things other than what they want to talk about because they see them as the denizens of the periphery of human society, they would work to decide for them what their agenda should be. In Durban, there was resistance to all that[88] and that course should be sustained with resilience.

[85] Mary Robinson, in an address during the eighteenth session of the Working Group of experts on People of African descent, held in Geneva from 11–15 April 2016.

[86] See Bakan and Bakan (2017), p. 228.

[87] Written statement by H.E. Mr. Thabo Mbeki, President of the Republic of South Africa, Annex IV, Report of the World Conference against Racism, https://www.oas.org/dil/afrodescendants_durban_declaration.pdf, p. 165.

[88] Ibid.

Consensus at Durban surprised certain circles and they are still working to give effect to their overtaken prediction prospectively. The inherent risk of racism and racial discrimination as highlighted by the authors of this book is the imbalance between political undertones and the substantive matters. Could this be inevitable considering that racism and racial discrimination are still found to be institutional, systemic and structured in the corpus of states and governments. The challenge for humanity is to confront the political challenges with rationality and break free. Advocate Gumbi emphasises the appeal to determine the impulses of our time. 'We need to put on the table, the impulses that are hindering us from implementing the decisions made at Durban and engage with them in the most honest way. We need to find the solutions to the challenges we are facing today'. The countries that are ready are leading the way with reforms to eradicate racism, racial discrimination, xenophobia, and all other forms of intolerances. It is a noble stance not to be led by disappointing dissent.

References

A Discussion on the U.N. World Conference Against Racism (house.gov), hearing before the subcommittee on International Operations and Human Rights of the Committee on International Relations House of Representatives, 107th Congress, First Session, 31 July 2001. Accessed 13 June 2025

Address of the President of South Africa, Thabo Mbeki, at the Opening of the World Conference Against Racism, Racial Discrimination, Xenophobia and Related Intolerance, Durban, 31 August 2001 | OHCHR. Accessed 15 June 2025

Bakan AB, Bakan YA (2017) Intersectionality and the World Conference against Racism. Atlantis 38(1):220–235

Camponovo CN (2003) Disaster in Durban: The United Nations World Conference against Racism, Racial Discrimination, Xenophobia and Related Intolerance. George Wash Int Law Rev 34:659

Contribution to the World Conference against Racism, Racial Discrimination, Xenophobia and Related Intolerance | EUR-Lex (europa.eu). Accessed 14 June 2025

Council Conclusions on the World Conference against Racism, Racial Discrimination, Xenophobia and Related Intolerance. General Affairs Council - 16 July 2001. Accessed 13 June 2025

Foreign Affairs Portfolio Committee, World Conference against Racism, 28 March 2001. World Conference Against Racism: Briefing by Department | PMG. Accessed 13 June 2025

General Conclusions of the European Conference against Racism, 16 October 2000. https://tandis.odihr.pl/explore?bitstream_id=22317&handle=20.500.12389/19346&provider=iiif-image#?c=0&m=0&s=0&cv=1&xywh=2180%2C144%2C2939%2C1360. Accessed 14 June 2025

McDougall G (2002) The World Conference against Racism: through a wider lens. Fletcher Forum World Aff 26(2):135–151

NGO Forum Declaration for the World Conference against Racism, Racial Discrimination, Xenophobia and other forms of Intolerance, 03 September 2001. Accessed 14 June 2025

Oosterlinck K et al (2022) A debt of dishonor. Boston Univ Law Rev 102:1248

Pillay shocked by US withdrawal from Durban Review Conference | OHCHR, Press Releases, Office of the High Commissioner for Human Rights, 19 April 2009. Accessed 14 June 2025

Plenary meeting of the World Conference Statement by Mary Robinson, High Commissioner for Human Rights and Secretary-General of the World Conference against Racism, Racial Discrimination, Xenophobia and Related Intolerance | OHCHR. Accessed 13 June 2025

Press Briefing by Chairman of Drafting Committee, 06 September 2001. Accessed 13 June 2025

Regional Meeting on Anti-Racism, FOCUS, March 2001, Vol. 23. Accessed 14 June 2025

Report of the Main Committee paras 17–19, pp. 110–111, annexed to the Report of the World Conference against Racism, Racial Discrimination, Xenophobia and Related Intolerance. Durban, 31 August–08 September 2001, A/CONF.189/2

Report of the Preparatory Committee on its First Session, U.N. GAOR, Hum. Rts. Comm., 1st Sess., U.N. Doc. A/CONF.189/PC.1/21 (2000), available at http://www.unhchr.ch/huridocda/huridoca.nsf/ (Symbol) /A.CONF. I 89.PC. 1.21 .En?Opendocument [hereinafter *First PrepCom]*

Report of the Regional Conference for Africa [in preparation for the World Conference against Racism, Racial Discrimination, Xenophobia and Related Intolerance], Dakar, 22–24 January 2001., https://digitallibrary.un.org/record/439789?ln=ar&v=pdf. Accessed 14 June 2025

Report of the World Conference against Racism, Racial Discrimination, Xenophobia and Related Intolerance. Durban, 31 August–08 September 2001, A/CONF.189/2, 0221543E (oas.org). Accessed 13 June 2024

Situation in the Democratic Republic of Congo in the case of the Prosecutor v Thomas Lubanga Dyilo, Decision establishing the principles and procedures to be applied to reparations, ICC-01/04-01/06, 07 August 2012

Statement by Chilean Minister of Planning and Cooperation_ Mrs Alejandra Krauss, World Conference against Racism, Racial Discrimination, Xenophobia and other related Intolerances. <https://www.un.org/WCAR/statements/chilE.htm>. Accessed 13 June 2025

Statement by Secretary-General on Conclusion of World Conference Against Racism, Racial Discrimination, Xenophobia and Related Intolerance, 08 September 2001. Accessed 14 June 2025

Sudan Claims Resolution Act, Dec. 2022., Accessed from https://www.gao.gov/assets/gao-23-105782.pdf. Accessed 13 June 2025

Summary of report on regional meetings. Accessed from https://www.unic.un.org.pl/durban/regional1.pdf. Accessed 14 June 2025

United Nations Millenium Declaration, General Assembly Resolution 55/2, 08 September 2000. Accessed 13 June 2025

World Conference against Racism, Racial Discrimination, Xenophobia and Related Intolerance: Declaration and Programme of Action, 2001

A Retrospective of the 2001 World Conference Against Racism

Gay J. McDougall

1 Introduction

The Durban Declaration and Programme of Action (DDPA) marked a historic effort to reorient the UN system and the approaches that had been taken by member states to combat racism, racial discrimination, xenophobia, and related intolerance.[1] The DDPA places in a common historical and structural context, issues of colonialism, the Trans-Atlantic Slave Trade, chattel slavery, xenophobia, and racism. It shifts the

Vice-Chair of the UN Committee on the Elimination of Racial Discrimination and Distinguished Scholar in Residence at Fordham University School of Law, New York, United States of America.

[1] The process of the 2001 World Conference against racism began in 1997 when the UN General Assembly convened a process, through General Assembly Resolution (A/RES/52/111) of 12 December 1997 that consisted of years of preparatory meetings, working groups, and advanced studies. The process culminated with several parallel conferences in Durban, South Africa, including the NGO Conference, held from August 28 to September 1, 2001, and the United Nations Governmental Conference, held from August 31 to September 8, 2001. The Governmental Conference was originally scheduled to end on September 7, 2001. However, due to the difficulty of resolving language concerning reparations and the Middle East, the World Conference was extended one day, until September 8, so that a consensus text could be finalized. The World Conference Secretariat published the final "Declaration and Programme of Action" on January 3, 2002 (A/CONF.189/12), and on March 27, the United Nations General Assembly adopted Resolution 56/266 supporting the outcome of the World Conference and calling for the full implementation of its Declaration and Programme of Action.

G. J. McDougall (✉)
UN Committee on the Elimination of Racial Discrimination | Fordham University School of Law, New York, NY, USA

C. S. Namakula (ed.), *Untold Reflections from the World Conference Against Racism*, SpringerBriefs in Law, https://doi.org/10.1007/978-3-032-17265-5_5

understanding of these scourges to being rooted in systems of economic gain. And it makes clear the importance of attacking the persistent structural remnants of those systems to reckon with contemporary racism and intolerance.

The DDPA further links racism, racial discrimination, xenophobia, and related intolerance to contemporary issues of economic and political inequality and provides an actionable agenda for combatting discrimination and intolerance embedded in societal institutions. In addition to highlighting the many racial, ethnic, and groups subject to racism and xenophobia, the DDPA is also among the first international human rights instruments to use explicitly the concept of "intersectional discrimination" to highlight the interlocking effects of gender, class, and related structures on the lived experience of racism.

The DDPA, also deserves mention as a core anti-racism instrument. It gave birth to new and important mechanisms, which seek to monitor implementation of the government commitments reached in Durban. Among them are the Inter-Governmental Working Group on the Effective Implementation of the DDPA, the Group of Independent Eminent Experts on the Implementation of the DDPA, the Working Group of Experts on People of African Descent and the Ad Hoc Committee on the Elaboration of Complementary Standards.

2 The Merits and Compromises of the Process of the 2001 World Conference Against Racism

In thinking about the Durban World Conference against Racism, it is important to keep in mind two points. First, world conferences are a process of dialogue and engagement that stretches over two or more years, culminating in the primary event and then proceeding through post-conference implementation. It is a journey, not simply a destination, during which relationships are built, perspectives are communicated, positions are changed, compromises are negotiated, and consensus emerges. Propelled by the process of the World Conference against Racism, practically every nation in the world discussed the causes and solutions to racial discrimination for over two years. There were many achievements gained during that process, even before we reached Durban.

The second point to keep in mind is that, in Durban, there were really several conferences taking place simultaneously on largely parallel tracks. Besides the official United Nations inter-governmental conference, there was the Voices Special Forum; daily public hearings of the testimony of victims of racial discrimination as it manifested in the twenty-first century. There was also the NGO Forum, and numerous workshops on a variety of issues, spread out in a geographic area that stretched to surrounding cities. The United Nations inter-governmental conference was largely unaware of developments taking place in the other venues. Depending on which conference one attended, his/her experiences of Durban might have varied greatly.

That said, I would make the following summary of what was accomplished at the World Conference against Racism:

- We grappled with the past in what was a historic discourse.
- We made an important statement about what racism looks like in the twenty-first century.
- We expanded the knowledge base about contemporary issues relating to racial discrimination.
- We re-affirmed some of humanity's most profound legal principles (equality and non-discrimination based on race), re-committed ourselves as a global community to them, and elaborated their meaning in this new era.
- We made plans for action around common ground.
- We identified the thorny issues around which there must be further dialogue, understanding, and struggle.
- We acknowledged the importance of civil society in the struggle against racism and gave birth to new global networks of civil society groups working to combat racism.
- We created a context that empowered a variety of victim groups.

Below I will expand upon a few of these points.

The World Conference against Racism, as many have aptly noted, was in part about who will bear the burden of history. The Trans-Atlantic Slave Trade and the era of colonialism were cataclysmic events that generated notions of racial inferiority as critical elements of their survival. The Durban Conference was the first global diplomatic forum that attempted to grapple with these past realities. It was a historic exchange of views.

The objective, first and foremost, was to make an honest assessment of the past and its legacy in the present. Without such retrospection, designing effective corrective measures is nearly impossible. Some governments wanted these past practices to be declared international crimes that would give rise to liability for reparations. Some wanted an apology. Those states most identified as the perpetrators of these historical events challenged the usefulness of focusing on the past.

The final language, accepted by consensus in the Durban Declaration and Programme of Action, moved the debate forward, despite its failure to satisfy fully any of the contesting positions. In the DDPA, governments acknowledge and express profound regret to those who suffered the effects of slavery, the slave trade, the Trans-Atlantic Slave Trade, apartheid, colonialism, and genocide.[2] Though not amounting to an apology, this language goes further than any previous international declaration in recognizing the gravity of these past wrongs, calling on the world community to remember these atrocities and to work to prevent them from

[2] World Conference Secretariat, "Declaration," para 99, "We acknowledge and profoundly regret the massive human sufferings and the tragic plight of millions of men, women and children caused by slavery, slave trade, Transatlantic Slave Trade, apartheid, colonialism and genocide and call upon States to honour the memory of the victims of past tragedies and affirm that wherever and whenever these occurred, they must be condemned and their reoccurrence prevented."

recurring. Governments, for the first time, recognized that slavery and slave trading are crimes against humanity and "should always have been so."[3]

Unfortunately, the compromise language in the Declaration falls short of acknowledging that the Trans-Atlantic Slave Trade constituted a crime against humanity at the time that it took place, largely because Western governments feared the implications that admission might have in litigation for reparations in national courts. The Conference failed to reach a consensus on declaring the system of colonialism to be an international crime.

These government declarations on the past are critical not only in their condemnation of slavery and colonialism, but also in the way they link these tragedies to the current-day problems of racism, racial discrimination, xenophobia, and related intolerance. Governments acknowledged that slavery and colonialism are root causes of contemporary racism and declared that the effects of slavery and colonialism continue to significantly impact the lives of descendants of victims today. The Declaration proclaims: "Africans and people of African descent, Asians and people of Asian descent, and indigenous peoples were victims of these acts and continue to be victims of their consequences."[4] Governments affirmed that the political, socio-economic, and cultural practices and structures of colonialism have contributed to contemporary forms of racism, racial discrimination, xenophobia, and related intolerance.[5]

With respect to the contentious issue of reparations, a compromise was fashioned, which some representatives of Non-Governmental Organizations thought created an unhelpful division between the interests of African states and the aspirations of the African Diaspora in the Americas. Governments recognized and reaffirmed the right of individual victims (presumably in the Diaspora) to seek reparations in their national courts.[6] No comment was made on the legitimacy of such claims with respect to the Trans-Atlantic Slave Trade.

At the international level, the claim for reparations was channeled into a discourse on development assistance.[7] The Programme of Action recognizes that the historical injustices discussed at the Durban Conference underlie the current economic disparities but avoids going further to imply legal or moral obligation. It gives its approval to a variety of forms of development assistance. The forms listed in the Programme of Action represent nothing new, nor do they establish new funding levels, timetables, or target outcomes.

---

[3] World Conference Secretariat, "Declaration," para 13. This historic language dealing with "crimes against humanity" originated at the Santiago PrepCom, which forged an agreement over the continued objections of the United States and Britain ("Santiago Declaration," para 27–32).

[4] Ibid.

[5] Ibid para 14.

[6] Ibid para 104. In the Durban Declaration and Programme of Action, "African Diaspora" refers to people of African descent living in the Americas, largely as a consequence of the Transatlantic Slave Trade. See World Conference Secretariat, "Programme of Action," para 7.

[7] Ibid para 159.

The Declaration notes "that some States have taken the initiative to apologize and have paid reparations where appropriate, for grave and massive violations committed"[8] and calls on those that have not yet expressed remorse or presented apologies to find some way to contribute to the restoration of the dignity of the victims.[9] There is no direct link made between regret for the past and the requirement to pay monetary compensation, although a "moral obligation" is cited to take appropriate steps to address the lasting consequences.[10] As Dr Zuma, President of the Durban Conference and South Africa's Minister of Foreign Affairs, summarized in her closing speech, "we agreed that slavery is a crime against humanity and that an apology is necessary, not for monetary gain, but to restore the dignity and humanity of those who suffered."[11] The very fact that governments seriously engaged in a discussion on reparations, however, established a benchmark for the reparations dialogue that would serve as a platform for further advancement of the issue. Perhaps most important, the Declaration affirms that "telling the truth about history [is an] essential element for international reconciliation and the creation of societies based on justice, equality and solidarity…."[12]

The process of the World Conference against Racism also provided a snapshot of racism in the twenty-first century. The face of racial discrimination has changed significantly since the International Convention on the Elimination of all Forms of Racial Discrimination (ICERD) was adopted in 1965.[13] Apartheid has ended in South Africa and colonialism has largely been defeated. Radical changes in the global economic system have forced massive population migrations from former colonial countries to northern industrialized metropolises. Today, first and second-generation migrant communities make racial equality an issue of domestic concern for practically all nations. But the majority of countries have either been in denial of that reality or have tried to stem the tide of migrants through restrictive immigration laws.

In Durban, and in the regional Preparatory Conferences (PrepComs)which preceded the main conference, the World Conference process changed that mentality. Governments declared that the fight against racism is an international priority for *all* nations in this third millennium.[14] Racism exists now in practically every country.

[8] World Conference Secretariat, "Declaration," para 100.

[9] Ibid., par. 101.

[10] Ibid., par. 102.

[11] Statement by H.E. Ms. Nkosazana Dlamini Zuma, Minister of Foreign Affairs of the Republic of South Africa and President of the World Conference, in Report of the World Conference against Racism, Racial Discrimination, Xenophobia, and Related Intolerance, A/CONF.189/12, p. 150.

[12] World Conference Secretariat, "Declaration", para 106.

[13] Adopted and opened for signature and ratification by General Assembly resolution 2106 (XX) of 21 December 1965. Entered into force, 4 January 1969 in accordance with Article 19.

[14] World Conference Secretariat, "Declaration" para 3, "We recognize and affirm that at the outset of the third millennium, a global fight against racism, racial discrimination, xenophobia and related intolerance, and all their abhorrent and evolving forms and manifestations is a matter of priority for the international community".

Governments agreed to focus on their own national laws and practices and to recognize, where, not if, racism is present within their borders. As former Amnesty International Secretary General Pierre Sané, observed, "It was an extraordinary admission by those who took part that racism exists in all societies."[15] Governments pledged to not only address obvious *de jure* forms of discrimination, but to scrutinize the policies and practices within their countries to ensure that *de facto* manifestations of racism are also understood and corrected.

One of the significant *lacunae* of the ICERD is that by its terms it appears to explicitly exempt application to how governments treat non-citizens. While the Committee on the Elimination of all Forms of Racial Discrimination (CERD), the Committee that oversees compliance with the ICERD, has addressed this apparent *lacunae* in its General Recommendations and practice with respect to its examination of State Parties to CERD,[16] the contemporary importance of the issue requires more direct treatment. The Durban Declaration notes "that xenophobia against non-nationals, particularly migrants, refugees and asylum-seekers, constitutes one of the main sources of contemporary racism."[17] UN High Commissioner for Human Rights and Secretary-General of the World Conference Mary Robinson commented that the Durban final document is "the best text internationally on migrants."[18]

The Durban Conference also emphasized the fact that "poverty, underdevelopment, marginalization, social exclusion, and economic disparities are closely associated with racism, racial discrimination, xenophobia and related intolerance."[19] The World Bank confirmed this conclusion in its assessment of Durban before the fifty-eighth session of the UN Human Rights Commission. The World Bank noted that racism and racial discrimination keep people in poverty, lead to a loss in personal and social security, and destroy the social fiber and fundamental dimensions of diversity. The World Bank thus agreed to work to assist any developing country trying to eliminate racial discrimination.[20]

Other contemporary manifestations of racism and racial discrimination detailed in the Durban Declaration and Programme of Action include such topics as HIV/

[15] Sané (2002). https://unesdoc.unesco.org/ark:/48223/pf0000123746. Accessed 18 May 2025.

[16] General Recommendation XI, (1993) and General Recommendation XXX on discrimination against non-citizens (Sixty-fourth session, 2004), U.N. Doc. CERD/C/64/Misc.11/rev.3 (2004).

[17] World Conference Secretariat, "Declaration," par. 16.

[18] Faheem (2002).

[19] World Conference Secretariat, "Declaration," par. 19.

[20] Statement by Alfredo Sfeir-Younis, Special Representative to the United Nations and the World Trade Organization, The World Bank, Fifty-Eighth Session of the Commission on Human Rights, 21 March 2002, Geneva, Item 6.

AIDS,[21] the Internet and media,[22] genetic research,[23] globalization,[24] and the intersection of racial discrimination with other forms of discrimination, notably with respect to race and gender, which creates unique experiences.[25]

The process of the Durban Conference generated the establishment, by the UN and other organizations, of special research bodies and working groups, and brought experts together on many occasions to critically analyze present day manifestations of racism. Specialized agencies such as the International Labor Organization (ILO) contributed studies and projects on the connections between racism and the world of work.[26] The United Nations Development Fund for Women (UNIFEM) produced studies on the intersection between race and gender. And NGOs provided hundreds of research and analytical reports on particular aspects of racism, racial discrimination, xenophobia, and related intolerance.

The Office of the UN Commissioner for Human Rights organized Regional Expert Seminars in five different regional meetings over the course of 2000.[27] The seminar groups, each composed of ten experts, presented papers and studies that identified and analyzed particular priorities, obstacles, and plans of action to combat racism in their region.[28] The result of these seminars was the creation of an expanded database about current forms and issues of racism.

Before the General Assembly convened the process of the World Conference against Racism, for example, there was very little data or analyses of ethnic conflict as an issue of relevance to racial discrimination in Africa. The expert seminar in Addis Ababa, however, focused solely on this issue and issued a report that provided substantive data on, among other issues, the causes, origins, and factors contributing to inter-communal tensions; the realization of economic, social, and cultural rights and the right to development as a strategy for the prevention of ethnic conflict; and

[21] World Conference Secretariat, "Declaration," par. 75; "Programme of Action," paras 3, 101, 110, 154, 158.

[22] World Conference Secretariat, "Declaration," paras 88–94; Programme of Action, paras 3, 43, 63, 86, 117, 119, 136, 140–147.

[23] Programme of Action para 73.

[24] World Conference Secretariat, "Declaration," paras 11, 12, 105; "Programme of Action," paras 96, 152, 209.

[25] World Conference Secretariat, "Declaration," para 69; "Programme of Action," paras 18, 31, 50–52, 54, 59, 63, 66, 94, 133, 136, 139, 176, 213.

[26] Other Questions: Preparations for the World Conference Against Racism, Racial Discrimination, Xenophobia and Related Intolerance, International Labor Office, Committee on Legal Issues and International Labour Standards, GB.280/LILS/12, 280th session, Geneva 2001. <l https://webapps.ilo.org/public/english/standards/relm/gb/docs/gb280/pdf/lils-12.pdf>. Accessed 14 June 2025.

[27] UN Human Rights Commission Resolution 2000/14, requesting that "the regional preparatory processes identify trends, priorities and obstacles at the national and regional levels, to formulate specific recommendations for the action to be carried out in the future to combat racism, racial discrimination, xenophobia and related intolerance and to submit to the Preparatory Committee, by its 2001 session at the latest, the conclusions of these regional preparatory processes."

[28] Summary of report on regional meetings. Accessed from https://www.unic.un.org.pl/durban/regional1.pdf. Accessed 14 June 2025.

the effectiveness of inter-national norms, mechanisms, and approaches to the prevention of ethnic and racial conflicts.[29]

The particular interplay between globalization and racism was another topic that had not been subject to significant studies or reports. In preparing for the Durban Conference, however, the United Nations Research Institute for Social Development (UNRISD) assessed how racism and inequality may be linked to the way labor markets are structured and differential access to government institutions.[30]

The process of the World Conference against Racism led institutions like the World Bank and the Inter-American Development Bank to generate studies for the first time on the plight of African descendant communities in Latin America. Critical data was also produced on the issue of trafficking in persons. Though much research had been done on this topic, it was the World Conference process that prompted the unique analysis of the racial implications of trafficking. These are just a few areas where our database of knowledge on contemporary forms of racism grew exponentially as a result of the Durban Conference.

The Durban Conference made forward-looking plans for action around common ground. Following the articulation of a set of general principles, governments committed themselves to a detailed programme of action with concrete commitments at the national, regional, and international level. Specifically, as Mary Robinson stated, governments pledged national plans and programs for 1) better treatment of victims; 2) tougher anti-discrimination legislation and administrative measures, which address both *de facto* as well as *de jure* forms of discrimination;[31] 3) universal ratification and implementation of ICERD and other relevant international treaties;[32] 4) strengthening education;[33] and 5) improving the remedies and recourses available to victims.[34]

In the Programme of Action, States made commitments to, among other things: review their existing national laws and policies, and where necessary, amend their national legislation, administrative procedures, and even their constitutions in order to foster equality among all individuals;[35] to design and fully implement effective policies and programs to prevent, detect, and ensure accountability for misconduct by police officers and other law enforcement personnel which is motivated by racism;[36] to eliminate racial profiling;[37] to promote a high quality and diverse police

[29] Addis Ababa Regional Seminar (A/CONF.189/PC.2/4).

[30] A detailed description of UNRISD's work before and during the World Conference can be found on their website, at Conference News: Racism and Public Policy. https://www.unrisd.org/en/library/publications/conference-news-racism-and-public-policy. Accessed on 18 May 2025.

[31] World Conference Secretariat, "Programme of Action," paras 66–74.

[32] Ibid paras 75–83.

[33] Ibid paras 117–139.

[34] Ibid paras 157–166.

[35] Ibid para 70.

[36] Ibid para 71.

[37] Ibid para 72.

force free from racism;[38] to prevent genetic research or its application from being used to promote racism and to prevent genetic information from being used for racist purposes;[39] to offer special protection for domestic workers, who in most countries are overwhelmingly women of color, and trafficked persons;[40] and to collect, disseminate, and publish reliable statistical data, disaggregated by race, to assess and monitor the situation of victims of racism and marginalized groups and to evaluate corrective measures.[41]

The successes of the Durban Conference may be best reflected in the way it empowered victim groups. The journey to Durban created an opportunity for victim groups around the world, many struggling with the invisibility of their cause, to articulate their issues to the world community and to engage their governments in a manner they had not been able to in the past. The World Conference process offered opportunities for building coalitions, sharing experiences, gaining strength, and strategizing. Groups representing the Roma, the African- Descendant communities in Latin America, migrants, and the Dalits felt that the World Conference focused world attention on their issues, created allies for their cause, galvanized their grassroots movements and produced concrete advances in their circumstances.

In the case of people of African descent in Latin America, the empowerment was substantial. In September 2000, one-year prior to the Durban Conference, South American governments, in a regional heads of state meeting, did not acknowledge the plight of the over 100 million African Descendants living in Latin America. The Durban Conference, however, provided the opportunity for this overlooked population to coordinate and mobilize. The results were dramatic. Today, affirmative action laws have been adopted in Brazil, which has the largest population of African Descendants in the Americas. Regionally, The Inter- American Development Bank, The Inter-American Dialogue, and the World Bank initiated the first Inter-Agency Consultation on Race Relations in Latin America (IAC). The IAC is designed to effectively address the special problems affecting African Descendant populations. The Inter-American Commission on Human Rights held hearings on African Descendants, which led to the decision to develop a regional convention on racial discrimination.

---

[38] Ibid para 74.

[39] Ibid para 73.

[40] Ibid para 69.

[41] Ibid paras 92–97.

3 Criticisms of the Durban Conference

Even considering the positive outcomes, some critics sought to delegitimize the Durban Conference and its outcomes. The aspect most criticized was the way the issue of the Israeli- Palestinian conflict was addressed during the last several months leading up to and including the final meeting in Durban.

These critics argue that the Israeli-Palestinian conflict should not have been an issue of debate at a conference on racial discrimination, that once it emerged on the agenda, ineffective efforts were taken to prevent it from spiraling out of control, that the debate ultimately became anti-Semitic, and that consequently, the Conference failed its primary mandate of combating racism. However, these arguments do not reflect the standard practices of global conferences or the facts of how this issue emerged and was treated at the 2001 UN World Conference.

First, the issue was appropriate for debate. It is hard to sustain the view that these were issues that had no relevance to the anti-discrimination agenda of the Conference or that to debate them was intrinsically anti-Semitic.[42]

Racism certainly exists in Israel just as it exists in practically every other country in the world. There are no grounds for exempting Israel from the same scrutiny of its policies and practices to which all other states are subject. As Pierre Sané notes in his assessment of Durban, "For delegations from Arab and Muslim countries, the [issue of the Palestinian/Israeli conflict] is one of human rights, discrimination, violence against a people, and a violation of the right to self-determination."[43] We must distinguish between a discourse that is critical of Israeli government policy and the articulation of views that are anti-Semitic. To blur these distinctions is not helpful or honest.

Second, Mary Robinson, as High Commissioner and Secretary General of the Conference, made numerous attempts to constructively manage the debate at the government conference.[44]

Of course, the most noticeable event in this regard was the "walk-out" of the United States and Israel, an action that had questionable impact on the final outcome. The United States had never been a full supporter of the Conference and had entered the process reluctantly under pressure from its African American constituency.[45] It played the role of the "doubting Thomas" throughout the first year and a

[42] The most vociferous critic, Congressman Tom Lantos, deemed the World Conference Against Racism worse than a failure he called it a reflection of the hatred that inspired the terrorist attacks on the United States a few days after the conference closed.

[43] Sané, note 14 above, 11.

[44] For instance, Mary Robinson chose not to just merge all of the regional drafts together, which would have included the contentious paragraphs of the Tehran document. Rather, she decided the most productive way to handle the compilation of regional drafts was to only include points of agreement into the working draft, thereby allowing the states to determine the placement of contentious issues.

[45] Initially, State Department support for the Durban conference was negative because of threats by Senator Jesse Helms to condition funding for the State Department and UN dues on there being no

half of the process, never fully committing itself to guaranteeing the success of the Conference. Additionally, as soon as the critique of Israeli policies first emerged in the Tehran PrepCom draft, there was an aggressive lobby from sectors within the Jewish-American community for the U.S. government to withdraw. By the time participants arrived in Durban, the U.S. walkout had been threatened for so long that it was anti-climactic when it actually happened.

Further, as stated earlier, events that took place in the NGO Forum were separate and largely unaffected by discussions in the official UN governmental conference. NGO Forums are encouraged and facilitated by the UN, but the UN takes no responsibility for setting the NGO agenda or for the final content of the closing documents.

At the same time, there were significant numbers of NGOs that raised legitimate and appropriate concerns about Israel's policies with respect to Palestinians in the occupied territories and within Israel proper.

Representatives of major sectors of the NGO community and the high commissioner denounced any anti-Semitic speech and activities that took place. The High Commissioner even rejected paragraphs in the final NGO text and took the unprecedented step of not endorsing the final NGO document to be transmitted to the government conference.[46] Such facts fly in the face of statements made by critics that neither the High Commissioner nor NGOs "did almost nothing to denounce the activities of the radicals in their midst".[47]

The vast majority of NGO representatives participating in the NGO Forum came with legitimate anti-racism agendas. The closing document from the NGO Forum is overwhelmingly progressive and articulates the aspirations of civil society groups from around the globe—people who face racism in their daily lives and who have much to say about how to combat it. With limited exceptions, the NGO Forum closing declaration is a valuable document for this reason.

---

support for future UN global conferences (See Public Law 106-113, 11/29/99). Later the administration of President Clinton established an Inter-Agency Task Force on the WCAR and conducted outreach programs in the civil rights community. But these were tentative steps that were quickly threatened when the issue of reparations for slavery was raised. Support from the Bush administration was even more lukewarm, in spite of the encouraging meetings between Secretary of State Colin Powell and the high commissioner for human rights.

[46] In a press briefing on Tuesday, September 5, Mrs. Robinson reiterated that she did not support "inappropriate content of the NGO Forum Declaration" and stated "for the first time, I can't recommend to dele gates to pay close attention to the document like I normally do." Daily Mail & Guardian, Durban, "Divisive NGO Declaration handed in at WCAR," Thursday, August 30, 2001.

[47] Lantos (2002), p. 43.

4 Conclusion

From its conception it was clear that the Third World Conference against Racism was not going to be an easy endeavor. The prior two conferences focused on matters such as apartheid that countries could more safely treat as foreign policy.[48] Those earlier conferences, however, were equally difficult. The Durban Conference was the first time a global meeting of this type sought to discuss racism, not as a foreign policy matter, but as a scourge that exists in every country and in all societies. No government really wanted to have this discussion. But, in spite of the reluctance of governments to consider domestic issues in international forums, and in spite of the many other obstacles placed in the way, the Durban Conference did indeed tackle some issues of fundamental importance to ending racism.

What we gained in Durban was an expression of determination, a commitment to equality expressed by a vast majority of the world's states. Governments re-affirmed some of humanity's most profound legal principles (equality and non-discrimination based on race), re-committed themselves as a global community to those principles and elaborated their meaning in this new era. It was a "moral re-armament"[49] for a struggle against one of the world's most intractable problems. This is the time to champion these renewed commitments.

References

Faheem K (2002) The education of Mary Robinson: a conversation with the UN's High Commissioner for Human Rights The Village Voice 20–30 April 2002

General Recommendation XI, (1993) and General Recommendation XXX on discrimination against non-citizens (Sixty-fourth session, 2004), U.N. Doc. CERD/C/64/Misc.11/rev.3 (2004)

International Convention on the Elimination of all Forms of Racial Discrimination (ICERD), adopted on 21 December 1965, entered into force, 4 January 1969

Lantos T (2002) The Durban debacle: an insider's view of the UN World Conference against Racism. Fletcher Forum World Aff 26(1):31–52

Other Questions: Preparations for the World Conference Against Racism, Racial Discrimination, Xenophobia and Related Intolerance, International Labor Office, Committee on Legal Issues and International Labour Standards, GB.280/LILS/12, 280th session, Geneva 2001. <lils-12.pdf>. Accessed 14 June 2025

Report of the World Conference to Combat Racism and Racial Discrimination, Geneva, 14–25 August 1978, A/CONF 92/40

Report of the World Conference against Racism, Racial Discrimination, Xenophobia and Related Intolerance. Durban, 31 August–08 September 2001, A/CONF.189/2, 0221543E (oas.org). Accessed 13 June 2024

[48] See Report of the World Conference to Combat Racism and Racial Discrimination, Geneva, 14–25 August 1978, A/CONF 92/40 and Report of the Second World Conference to Combat Racism and Racial Discrimination, Geneva, 1–12 August 1983, A/CONF./119/26.

[49] Sané, note 14 above, 11.

Report to the Second World Conference to Combat Racism and Racial Discrimination, Geneva, 1–12 August 1983, A/CONF./119/26

Sané P (2002) In defence of Durban: racism is back on the agenda - UNESCO Digital Library. Accessed 18 May 2025

Statement by Alfredo Sfeir-Younis, Special Representative to the United Nations and the World Trade Organization, The World Bank, Fifty-Eighth Session of the Commission on Human Rights, 21 March 2002, Geneva, Item 6

Summary of report on regional meetings. Accessed from https://www.unic.un.org.pl/durban/regional1.pdf, at p 12. Accessed 14 June 2025

World Conference against Racism, Racial Discrimination, Xenophobia and Related Intolerance: Declaration and Programme of Action, 2001

Durban Beyond 20: Reflections on Brazil's Participation at the World Conference Against Racism

Silvio J. Albuquerque e Silva

1 Introduction

In rare moments of Brazilian diplomatic action in human rights, foreign policy objectives and domestic policy priorities were aligned in the preparatory process and during the World Conference against Racism, Racial Discrimination, Xenophobia and Related Intolerance. Brazil did not simply play a supporting role in dealing with the Conference's central themes. Alongside other actors, Brazilian diplomacy played a central role in the most important international meeting organized by the United Nations Organization dedicated to the fight against one of the great wounds of humanity: discriminatory treatment against human beings based on racial criteria and other related forms of prejudice. The course of the meeting and most of its outcomes carry the fingerprint of Brazil's diplomatic endeavours and the active role played by the dynamic Brazilian civil society.

Ambassador of Brazil to the Kingdom of Belgium and the Grand Duchy of Luxembourg (since August 2025), Ambassador of Brazil to Kenya, Rwanda, Uganda, Burundi and Somalia, and Permanent Representative to the UN in Nairobi (2021–2025). Member of the United Nations Committee on the Elimination of Racial Discrimination (2018–2022). First Chair of the Working Group of the Organization of American States responsible for the Negotiation of the Inter-American Convention Against Racism, Racial Discrimination and Related Forms of Intolerance (2005–2006). Member of the Brazilian Delegation to the Durban Conference. Author of the books: "The United Nations and the International Fight Against Racism", FUNAG, Brasília, Third Edition, 2023, and "Environmental Multilateralism and Racial Discrimination", FUNAG, Brasilia, 2025.

S. J. Albuquerque e Silva (✉)
Brasília, Brazil

Luxembourg, Luxembourg

C. S. Namakula (ed.), *Untold Reflections from the World Conference Against Racism*, SpringerBriefs in Law, https://doi.org/10.1007/978-3-032-17265-5_6

The ideas contained in this essay reflect the author's personal position and not necessarily that of the Brazilian government. The fight against racial discrimination has constituted the 40 year career of the author as a diplomat, academic, an expert member of the Committee on the Elimination of Racial Discrimination (CERD), and as under-secretary of State for human rights of Brazil. I have never believed that the role of States and the United Nations in eliminating racism and racial discrimination is neutral. It was fortuitous, therefore, for a young diplomat to be presented with the chance of contributing to crucial moments of building the positions of the Brazilian government for the Durban Conference, from the beginning, and in permanent articulation with sectors of Brazilian civil society.

The measure of the importance of Durban for Brazil can be given by the reflection of the Brazilian Ambassador Gilberto Saboia, former Secretary of State of Human Rights (2000–2001), who said that the internal preparatory process for the Conference was positive in itself, regardless of the results of the world meeting. In fact, the national preparation provided the broadest discussion on the racial issue in the history of Brazil, ensuring great visibility to the central themes of the meeting among different segments of our society. The explicit recognition by the government of the existence of racism and racial discrimination in the country contributed decisively to the active participation of representatives of various sectors of civil society in the internal preparatory process and in the negotiations carried out in Santiago, Geneva and Durban.

The Brazilian domestic preparation gave rise to closer dialogue and collaboration between the government and non-governmental organizations dedicated to defending the rights of people of African descent, indigenous peoples, homosexuals and other minorities. New alliances were established between civil society entities committed to the fight against racism and discrimination. Statistical and diagnostic studies were conducted on the reality of discrimination in the country. The role of national institutions dedicated to promoting and protecting human rights was strengthened.

As a result of the Durban process, the promotion of equality and the fight against racism and discrimination were incorporated as one of Brazil's foreign policy priorities, in addition to having been integrated into the national political agenda and raised to the status of permanent State policy. In this sense, the legitimacy of the internal process of formulation and implementation of the Brazilian foreign policy was strengthened in the specific context of the Durban Conference, which was positively reflected in the performance of Brazil's delegation in South Africa.

It has always been a taboo to deal with the topic of racial discrimination in international relations. Unlike other topics on the international agenda, the decision to combat and overcome racism and discrimination originates within States and the two phenomena are perceived and faced by governments in different ways. With greater or lesser intensity, over the decades, different States have often reacted defensively to allegations of racism and racial discrimination in their societies. In doing so, they act as if international instruments specifically aimed at combating racial discrimination were an instrument of foreign policy, that is, affecting other countries and not their internal reality.

This distorted perception of reality, which guided many States that signed and ratified the International Convention on the Elimination of All Forms of Racial Discrimination,[1] was also present in the process of holding the Durban Conference, which brought with it the concrete possibility that governments were to be directly and publicly questioned about their practices. Furthermore, in a globalized world where frustrations with worsening inequality were multiplying, the Conference would be the natural point of confluence of demands whose scope could go beyond racism, xenophobia and intolerance. Despite these challenges and the criticisms that have been levelled at it, the Durban Conference achieved highly positive results. Its Declaration and Action Plan represents an anti-discrimination agenda that suggests concrete paths for the development of national strategies and articulation of policies for international organizations to combat racism, racial discrimination, xenophobia and related intolerance. It also symbolizes the vision of a world that welcomes diversity and clearly positions itself in favour of equality. In this sense, it is an antidote to negative stereotypes, which tend to fuel intolerance, hatred and violence.

The Durban outcome document has the virtue of taking advantage of the universalist conception of human rights, unlike certain anti-racism legislation or policies. The proposals contained in the Declaration and Plan of Action cannot be ignored during any objective reflection on national and international strategies to effectively combat racism, racial discrimination, xenophobia and intolerance. This document contains recommendations to states that must be complied with *ex bona fide*.

Whereas the Durban Declaration and Programme of Action (DDPA)[2] does not have automatic compulsory force over any State, its provisions can, over time, be cited as customary interpretations of international law and acquire some legal force. In particular, the DDPA provides (a) valuable consensus and commitments reached at the international level on the origins, causes, forms and contemporary manifestations of racism, racial discrimination, xenophobia and related intolerance, (b) clear identification of the victims of these practices and the effective reparation measures to their benefit, (c) prevention, education and protection measures aimed at eradicating racism and other evils at national and international levels, and (d) defined strategies to achieve full and effective equality. These strategies encompass international cooperation and strengthening the United Nations and other multilateral organizations in the fight against these scourges.

2 Brazilian Diplomacy in the Santiago Regional Preparatory Conference

To understand the central role of Brazilian diplomacy in the Durban Conference, it is first of all necessary to analyze the role the country played in the region, in preparation for Durban. The Regional Preparatory Conference of the Americas was held

[1] Adopted on 21 December 1965, entered into force, 4 January 1969.

[2] World Conference against Racism, Racial Discrimination, Xenophobia and Related Intolerance: Declaration and Programme of Action, 2001.

in Santiago (Chile), from the 5th to the 7th of December 2000.[3] It proceeded in an unprecedented format since it had the participation of all countries of the continent, including Canada and the United States, although both have always been part of the so-called "Western European and Others Group" (WEOG).

More than 1700 representatives of civil society participated in events parallel to the official meeting of States and governments. There were more than 170 representatives of Brazilian civil society, constituting the second largest delegation of NGOs, surpassed only by the approximately 400 Chilean representatives, mostly Mapuche indigenous people. The Citizens' Conference of Americas, held days before the governmental meeting (3 and 4 December 2000), resulted in a final declaration forwarded to the representatives of States.

Led by Ambassador Gilberto Saboia, the Brazilian delegation comprised of officials of federal government agencies and various representatives of the National Preparatory Committee from civil society, which included, *inter alia*, an impressive number of members of the Black Movement of Indigenous organizations, and entities representing movements of other racial, religious and sexual minorities. According to official instructions, universal representation of the different segments of Brazilian society demonstrated the willingness of the government of Brazil to (1) collaborate closely with the main stakeholders in the search for solutions to racism in Brazil, and (2) harness their experience towards formulating creative proposals that could help in obtaining consensus on the continent, crystallized in the Declaration and Plan of Action to be adopted in Santiago.

In a demonstration of the Brazilian State's commitment to the results of the Regional Conference, the official instructions emphasized that Brazil, a country with the largest contingent of the Black population outside Africa, an indigenous population, and descendants of immigrants from the most diverse origins, had credentials to demonstrate the positive effects of co-existence and tolerance, as well as a political aptitude to face the challenge of employing effective measures to combat persistent practices of racial discrimination that persisted in our society.

At the end of the intergovernmental negotiating process, it was possible to identify several conceptual advances in the Declaration and Plan of Action of Santiago[4] that resulted from positions conceived and defended by the Brazilian delegation. An example in this regard was the recognition in Article 11 of the Declaration that the victims of racism, racial discrimination, xenophobia and intolerance in the Americas were people of African descent and indigenous people, as well as other groups, such as migrant workers and their family members. The insertion of certain innovative concepts or principles in the Santiago document could also be considered a Brazilian diplomatic success. They include (1) recognition of the existence of a relationship between the legacy of slavery, the slave trade and colonialism and the contemporary

[3] Report of the Regional Conference of the Americas, Santiago, Chile, 5–7 December 2000: https://digitallibrary.un.org/record/440441?ln=en&v=pdf. Accessed 14 June 2025.

[4] Documents adopted by the Regional Conference of the Americas, held in Santiago de Chile, Chile from 5–7 December 2000: https://digitallibrary.un.org/record/431132?ln=en&v=pdf. Accessed 14 June 2025.

manifestations of racism; (2) recognition that the trafficking of enslaved people and similar forms of servitude could constitute crimes against humanity in the present day; (3) inclusion of sexual orientation as one of the grounds for discrimination; (4) the use of the expression: "indigenous peoples", even if associated with a safeguard clause, which qualifies the meaning of the term "peoples"; (5) the recognition of race, color, gender, age, religion, creed, sexual orientation, disability, among other grounds as multiple or aggravating factors of discrimination; (6) the importance of the adoption of affirmative action (special measures) as a form of historical reparation for discrimination suffered by individuals and groups; (7) the explicit recognition, by States, that racial discrimination was a problem in all countries of the Americas; (8) the condemnation of political platforms and organizations based on racism, discrimination, xenophobia and related intolerance, which constituted a threat to democracy; (9) the Programme of Action exhorted States to develop the Inter-American Convention against Racism, Racial Discrimination, Xenophobia and Related Intolerance within the framework of the Organization of American States.

3 Brazilian Diplomacy in Durban

The official Brazilian delegation to the Durban World Conference was among the biggest. The total of Brazilian official delegates including representatives of civil society organizations attending the event in South Africa approached 500. The delegation was led by Mr. José Gregori, the then Minister of Justice. Ambassador Gilberto Saboia was the alternate Head of delegation that included, *inter alia*, the State Governor of Alagoas, the Deputy Governor of Rio de Janeiro, a Senator, twelve Congressmen, one Justice from the Superior Court of Labor, a representative of the Federal Prosecutor's Office, in addition to members of the National Preparatory Committee, and the National Council of Women's Rights.

The delegation's composition reflected the degree of importance that the State and Brazilian society attributed to the central objectives of the Durban Conference. For the most part, delegates and representatives of Brazilian Non-Governmental Organizations held legitimate expectations of the possibility that Brazil would contribute balanced paragraphs on themes deemed of great importance by the National Preparatory Committee to the introduction in the Declaration and Plan of Action. Those themes included the discrimination suffered by the people of African descent, indigenous peoples and, in an aggravated form, by women, children and the LGBTQIA+ community.

The Brazilian diplomatic line of action was guided by the same cooperative and conciliatory spirit with which the country had acted throughout the entire regional preparatory process and international dialogue. Brazil's main objective was to help build an advanced text that objectively dealt with the historical causes of racism and clearly identified the victims of those manifestations. At the same time, it was in Brazil's interest that the Plan of Action contained objective and constructive language, which led to the adoption of concrete proposals to overcome the traditional ways and contemporary forms of racism, racial discrimination, xenophobia and related intolerance.

The official instructions indicated that, in relation to both questions of the past and those related to contemporary themes, Brazil should reject proposals towards the "selective condemnation of states". The understanding was that it would not be politically viable nor allow overcoming the obstacles created by some countries, especially those linked to the colonial legacy. The logic underlying this conciliatory position was the recognition that racism, racial discrimination, xenophobia and related intolerance were problems shared by all the states. In this sense, Brazil's view was that the link that united everyone in the Conference should be precisely the determination to solve those problems.

Brazil's delegation was able to act in a firm and determined manner, aiming to positively influence the difficult negotiations held in the scope of the Working Groups in charge of drafting the Declaration and Programme of Action. Throughout the entire meeting, the Brazilian performance would be marked by constant interaction and the fluidity of dialogue between government and civil society, maintaining the momentum set in the global preparatory sessions.

The choice of Ambassador Gilberto Saboia as facilitator of the informal group in charge of consensual drafting of paragraphs on the themes of the past and reparations, certainly one of the most important and complex aspects of the entire Conference, reflected Member States' recognition of the outstanding performance of the said diplomat and the Brazilian delegation during the international and regional preparatory meetings. Balanced and objective writing of the paragraphs agreed under Brazilian intermediation proved to be extremely constructive. The success of negotiations in relation to legacies of the past and reparation would represent one of the two occasions when the success of the Conference resulted from the direct action of Brazilian diplomacy.

The other Brazilian diplomatic initiative that was decisive for the success of the Conference was the one related to issues of the Middle East. Dissatisfied with the fact that the new paragraphs on the subject as presented by the Presidency of the Conference, were based on language more moderate than that used in the draft Declaration and Action Plan considered at the last Preparatory Committee meeting, the representative of Syria proposed that the Main Committee reconsidered three of the most controversial paragraphs of the draft. The Syrian delegate's proposal that was formulated on the last day of the Durban Conference, surprised most of the delegations and especially the Presidency of the Conference by generating what could have resulted in a catastrophic impasse of the works.

After the suspension of the plenary meeting for about 2 hours, the Brazilian representative, Ambassador Saboia, in an intelligent and courageous action aimed at saving the Conference, submitted a motion of non-consideration of the texts resubmitted by the Syrian delegation for consideration by the Plenary. Following the rules of procedure of the Conference,[5] the Brazilian motion would need the support of two delegations to be put to a vote in plenary. However, the skilful initiative of the Brazilian delegation was not understood by the various delegations that opposed the Syrian proposal. With that, the opposition of the motion by the delegations of Algeria and Syria forced Brazil to withdraw its proposal.

Realizing the importance and meaning of the Brazilian action, the representative of Belgium resubmitted the motion on behalf of the European Union. Representatives from Argentina and Russia made statements supporting the proposal. Delegates from South Africa and Syria opposed the motion. By request of the representative of Australia, a roll-call vote was held, which resulted in the adoption of the motion by 51 votes in favour (including Brazil), 37 against and 11 abstentions. Countries that supported the motion included the totality of those belonging to the Western Europe and Others Group and most of the East European Group delegations, the largest number of members of the Group of Latin America and Caribbean Countries (GRULAC) and three delegations of the African Group (Congo, Gabon and Ghana). Most of the votes against the motion came from delegations from the African and Asian Group and four countries from the GRULAC (Barbados, Cuba, Saint Vincent and the Grenadines, and Trinidad and Tobago). Those that abstained were Armenia, Azerbaijan, Bosnia and Herzegovina, Singapore, Ecuador, Philippines, India, Kenya, Senegal, Seychelles and Togo.

As for the main objectives achieved by the set of actions of Brazilian diplomats during the Conference, it is worth mentioning the recognition of people of African descent, indigenous peoples and people living with HIV, among others, as victims of racism, racial discrimination, xenophobia and related intolerance. In the case of people of African descent, the emphasis on the importance of their equal participation in the political, economic, social and cultural aspects of their societies was especially relevant. In addition, several paragraphs of the Plan of Action contain concrete and effective proposals to overcome the multiple obstacles faced by people of African descent. Concerning indigenous peoples, emphasis should be placed on the importance of consecrating the use of the term "peoples" as a denomination of reference to this human group by the states in international fora. In the case of individuals infected by the HIV/AIDS, the Declaration and Plan of Action mentioned the need for the States to adopt concrete measures to ensure appropriate access of patients to medicines. The inclusion of this theme in the Conference meant the reaffirmation of the concept present in a resolution titled "Access to Medicines in the Context of Pandemics such as HIV/AIDS" sponsored by Brazil and adopted by the then UN Commission on Human Rights.[6] Equally positive for Brazil was the reiteration of the importance of adopting special measures or affirmative action in favour of individuals and groups at risk of discrimination.

---

[5] (Provisional) Rules of Procedure of the Durban Conference, A/CONF.189/2 (14 August 2001), adopted on 31 August 2001. Available from: https://documents.un.org/doc/undoc/gen/g01/154/73/pdf/g0115473.pdf.

[6] Commission on Human Rights Resolution 2001/33. <E-CN_4-RES-2001-33.doc>. Accessed 14 June 2025.

In a statement made at the twentieth and last plenary session, held on 8th September 2001, under item 10 of the agenda of the global meeting (dubbed "Adoption of the Final Document and the Report of the Conference"), the Brazilian delegation emphasized that the Declaration and Programme of Action represented "a significant step in the fight against racism, racial discrimination, xenophobia and related intolerance". In addition to praising the advances represented by paragraphs concerning, *inter alia*, the themes of the past and on the People of African descent and indigenous peoples, the Brazilian representative regretted that the protection of the human rights of victims of aggravated discrimination had been restricted by the exclusion factors such as sexual orientation and gender. The inclusion of sexual orientation as one of the multiple factors of racial discrimination in the document was defended by the Brazilian delegation based on the recognition of the clearly unsatisfactory situation, from the human rights perspective, that part of humanity lives in all countries. Despite having the support of several delegations, especially from GRULAC and the WEOG, the Brazilian proposal to insert this issue in the text was rejected by an alliance comprising majorly of African and Asian countries, and the Vatican.

4 The Global Context for the Durban Conference

The Durban World Conference can be analyzed from at least two perspectives. The first would emphasize the counterpoint of interests, and the differences in the perceptions of certain States and some actors on a restricted universe of contentious issues related particularly to (1) the conflict in the Middle East; (2) the legacy of the slave trade; (3) the slave regime and colonialism and (4) the reparations due to victims of racism. The second perspective is an overall view of the breadth and multiplicity of topics addressed at the Conference. It is intended to identify the points of convergence in treating central issues by States, Regional Groups and international and non-governmental organizations.

The advantage of this last line of analysis is that it allows viewing the Durban Conference as a process of dialogue and multilateral negotiation that formally lasted over 10 years since the official convening of the event by the UN General Assembly in 1997.[7] It involved preparatory negotiations for approximately 2 years, culminated in the realization of the global event and has not ended yet. In fact, since then, it has continued through the actions of mechanisms for monitoring how the commitments agreed in South Africa are being redeemed by the States. This perspective also evaluates the historical performance of the United Nations in the fight against racism and racial discrimination and elevates a requirement that, in terms of human

[7] Third Decade to Combat Racism and Racial Discrimination and the Convening of a World Conference Against Racism, Racial Discrimination, Xenophobia and Related Intolerance, A/RES/52/111, 12 December 1997. Available from: http://www.worldlii.org/int/other/UNGA/1997/204.pdf.

rights, cannot be ignored: the notion of process, "in which change erupts despite the persistence of a continuous backdrop".

The vision of the Durban Conference as part of a process of change in the international strategy and in the attitude of the States toward confronting racism and related discrimination was clearly reflected in Kofi Annan's speech at the opening of the Conference. By stating that the event in South Africa was a test for the international community "of its willingness to unite around an issue of central importance in people's lives", he stressed that States could not afford to fail in the commitments to be agreed. The then UN Secretary-General pointed out that the preparation process had "provoked an extraordinary mobilization of civil society in several countries" and generated expectations that could not be ignored.

Over the past 60 years, the international system for the protection of human rights has developed based on the equality of all human beings in rights. Above these rights hovers the principle of human dignity, a true "super-principle" guiding both international and domestic law. For these reasons, the fight against racism, racial discrimination, xenophobia and related intolerance represents a specific and particular form of fight in favour of human rights.

Having built its foundations since the Universal Declaration of Human Rights in 1948,[8] it was only after the World Conference on Human Rights in Vienna in 1993[9] that human rights began to be recognized by the international community as universal, indivisible and interdependent.

Although the advances achieved in the field of human rights protection between the early 1990s and the present day have yet to produce profound and desirable transformations on a world scale, the Vienna Declaration established a new level for the multilateral treatment of the theme.[10] From the "spirit of Vienna" was born the proposal to convene a world meeting against contemporary racism, culminating into the cycle of world conferences held by the United Nations since 1990. Approved on 8/12/1994 by the so-called Sub-Commission on Prevention of Discrimination and Protection of Minorities, the resolution entitled "A World Conference against Racism, Racial or Ethnic Discrimination, Xenophobia and Other Related Contemporary Forms of Intolerance" proposed that the global event be held in the year 1997.[11] In 1995, the Commission on Human Rights endorsed the Sub-Commission's proposal, which would, in turn, be endorsed by the Economic and Social Council (ECOSOC) and forwarded it to the UN General Assembly. Only 2 years later, in 1997, the General Assembly gave the definitive endorsement to the holding of the Conference, which was renamed "World Conference Against Racism,

[8] https://www.un.org/sites/un2.un.org/files/2021/03/udhr.pdf Accessed 14 June 2025.

[9] World Conference on Human Rights, Vienna, 1993 | OHCHR. https://www.ohchr.org/en/about-us/history/vienna-declaration. Accessed 14 June 2025.

[10] Vienna Declaration and Programme of Action | OHCHR. https://www.ohchr.org/en/instruments-mechanisms/instruments/vienna-declaration-and-programme-action. Accessed 14 June 2025.

[11] See Report of the UN Sub-Commission on Prevention of Discrimination and Protection of Minorities on its 46th Session, U.N. Doc. E/CN.4/Sub.2/1994/56 (1994), 28 October 1994, para 1. https://hrlibrary.umn.edu/demo/1994min.html#IB1. Accessed 14 June 2025.

Racial Discrimination, Xenophobia and Related Intolerance". According to Resolution 52/11, it had to take place "not later than the year 2001".[12]

When the global meeting was convened, the international context favoured utilising multilateral diplomacy. With the crisis of multilateralism in the 1980s overcome, the last decade of the twentieth century witnessed the effects of East-West distension and the end of the Cold War. Several issues, relegated for decades to the restrictive competence of the States, emerged on the international agenda as global themes whose consensual treatment sought to rescue the value of human dignity, promote the common good, correct imbalances and prevent world instability. In addition to the States, civil society organizations began to act on the international scene, assuming increasingly central roles, especially in the areas of human rights and the environment.

At that historic moment, a set of circumstances justified the opportunity of holding a conference that addressed the issue of combating racism and racial discrimination from a planetary perspective, unlike what had happened at the world conferences against racism and racial discrimination in 1978 and 1983, focused on combating the apartheid regime in force in South Africa. The great political and historical fact of the first half of the 1990s was the end of South African apartheid in 1994, "a true absence of attention fixation by the evil that it brought within itself and as a threat to peace and security aggravated by the context of bipolar confrontation". Overcoming it would enable the international community to deal with the structural phenomenon of racism and racial discrimination, present, under different guises, in all countries of the world.

According to Kofi Annan, former UN Secretary-General, through the conference cycle of the 1990s, the United Nations played the harmonizing role envisioned in its founding Charter and served "as an indispensable forum in which different points of view were defended, proposals were debated and, most importantly, political consensus was reached".[13] As a result, the international community, States, intergovernmental and non-governmental organizations and civil society, was able to "set a new course for a new era in global affairs".[14] However, in the background of this optimistic scenario lay old and new antagonisms and prejudices, some of them with deep roots originating even before the Cold War period.

At the end of the 1990s, there was a widespread perception that, despite international efforts to contain racist ideologies and overcome racial discrimination, xenophobia and related intolerance, such manifestations were increasing in the world and gaining space in full heart of Europe, reinforced by political parties with demagogic, ultranationalist and xenophobic programmatic platforms. Added to this phenomenon is an extreme form of racism, the so-called "ethnic cleansing", which by victimizing millions of people in Africa (Rwanda) and tens of thousands in Europe (Yugoslavia), had demonstrated its devastating impact on human rights.

---

[12] A/RES/52/111, note 8 above, para 29 (a).

[13] Reitano (1999), p. 115.

[14] Ibid.

It was precisely that international scenario that surrounded the process of preparing and holding the World Conference in Durban. Contrary to what happened in the early 1990s, the first United Nations conference with a truly global scope to deal with the issue of racism and racial discrimination, in addition to two other related issues, would be held in a context of weakening the promises of multilateralism and of parliamentary diplomacy, partly as a result of the fact that the 189 Member States constituted a mesh of contradictory interests more complex than the game prevailing in the early 1990s. In addition, the central theme of Durban would prove to be of great sensitivity and discomfort for the countries of the European Union and, above all, for the United States, a country which, given its world hegemonic power, allowed itself to act, since the end of the Cold War, instrumentally and selectively at the multilateral level. For their part, several African countries would come to defend maximalist positions on issues linked to the past (slavery, the slave trade and colonialism) and the compensation eventually due to States and descendants of individual or collective victims of these practices.

The World Conference in Durban would place the United Nations in a minefield since, unlike other issues on the international agenda, racism and discrimination to be fought and overcome originate within States and are perceived and faced by governments in different ways. In other words, holding the Conference brought with it the concrete possibility that governments would be directly and publicly questioned about their practices. Furthermore, in a globalized world where frustrations with the worsening of inequality multiplied, the Conference would be the natural point of confluence of claims whose scope could go beyond racism, xenophobia and intolerance.

Despite these challenges and the criticism levelled at it, the Durban Conference achieved highly positive results. Its Declaration and Programme of Action represents an anti-discrimination agenda that suggests concrete paths for the development of national strategies and the articulation of international policies to combat racism, racial discrimination, xenophobia and related intolerance. It also symbolizes the vision of a world that welcomes diversity and is clearly positioned to favour equality. In this sense, it is an antidote against negative stereotypes, which tend to feed intolerance, hatred and violence. The Durban outcome document also has the virtue of using the universalist conception of human rights contrary to certain anti-racism legislation or policies.

5 Conclusion

Given the exponential growth of manifestations of discrimination and racial hatred in the world, in a few moments of history, the reaffirmation of the principles, rights and guarantees provided for in the International Convention on the Elimination of Racial Discrimination and the Durban Declaration and Programme of Action was so important. In the case of the Universal Declaration of Human Rights, its principles are universally accepted as an instrument that integrates international customary law and, at least in serious and systematic forms, the *jus cogens*. Regarding Durban's legacy, it is important to reject the superficial and partial view that refuses to recognize its conceptual advances, its diagnoses and, above all, its set of recommendations. Those who choose to focus on divergences rather than convergences do a disservice to the cause of human rights and the fight against racial discrimination.

It is essential to learn to listen carefully to the cries of victims of violence and arbitrary acts motivated by racism and by racial discrimination. In a certain way, by transforming the pain of others into fuel for the inevitable challenges in the field of human rights, we are respecting the logic of a social contract signed by the international community in 1948 and reaffirmed over the decades through the nine international conventions monitored by independent committees, and the results of international conferences on human rights and against racism and racial discrimination.

This civilizational pact, inaugurated in 1948, operates in two plans. One of them is that of the "here and now", in which the thirty articles of the Universal Declaration on Human Rights and the bulk of the rights and obligations enshrined in Conventions and other international documents establish the rules of the game and indirectly determine the lines of action. The other much deeper plan is the accumulation of forces that interspersed with victories and defeats, are the real provider of meaning to the "here and the now" and the legal-political space contained in the Declaration, Conventions and Durban outcome documents. This other dimension is a strange contract, not based on a written document. It is a contract between generations, mine and that of my children and grandchildren, that, in their coming, living and passing, update libertarian dreams and traditions. These will be the ones when realized at some point, will determine that the idea of progress, as Walter Benjamin's angel of history suggests, ceases to be synonymous with a storm.[15]

I close this text by remembering a mantra that accompanies me in several conversations I have had on the topic of racial discrimination lately. It has to do with the role of each one of us on an individual level and in our interpersonal relationships. It is time to reflect incisively on our complicity—sometimes involuntary—with everyday forms of violence and racism and react to the insensitivity of so many in the face of the suffering generated by racial discrimination.

Reports

'Access to Medicines in the Context of Pandemics such as HIV/AIDS' Commission on Human Rights Resolution 2001/33. <E-CN_4-RES-2001-33.doc>. https://view.officeapps.live.com/op/view.aspx?src=https%3A%2F%2Fap.ohchr.org%2

[15] Walter Benjamin on the Concept of History/Theses on the Philosophy of History. https://www.sfu.ca/~andrewf/CONCEPT2.html. Accessed 14 June 2025.

Fdocuments%2FE%2FCHR%2Fresolutions%2FE-CN_4-RES-2001-33.doc&wdOrigin=BROWSELINK. Accessed 14 June 2025.

Documents adopted by the Regional Conference of the Americas, held in Santiago de Chile, Chile from 5–7 December 2000. https://digitallibrary.un.org/record/431132?ln=en&v=pdf. Accessed 14 June 2025.

International Convention on the Elimination of All Forms of Racial Discrimination, Adopted on 21 December 1965, entered into force, 4 January 1969.

(Provisional) Rules of Procedure of the Durban Conference, A/CONF.189/2 (14 August 2001), https://documents.un.org/doc/undoc/gen/g01/154/73/pdf/g0115473.pdf, adopted on 31 August 2001.

Report of the Regional Conference of the Americas, Santiago, Chile, 5–7 December 2000. https://digitallibrary.un.org/record/440441?ln=en&v=pdf. Accessed 14 June 2025.

Report of the UN Sub-Commission on Prevention of Discrimination and Protection of Minorities on its 46th Session, U.N. Doc. E/CN.4/Sub.2/1994/56 (1994), 28 October 1994.

Third Decade to Combat Racism and Racial Discrimination and the Convening of a World Conference Against Racism, Racial Discrimination, Xenophobia and Related Intolerance, A/RES/52/111, 12 December 1997, http://www.worldlii.org/int/other/UNGA/1997/204.pdf.

Vienna Declaration and Programme of Action | OHCHR. https://www.ohchr.org/en/instruments-mechanisms/instruments/vienna-declaration-and-programme-action. Accessed 14 June 2025.

Walter Benjamin on the Concept of History/Theses on the Philosophy of History. https://www.sfu.ca/~andrewf/CONCEPT2.html. Accessed 14 June 2025.

World Conference against Racism, Racial Discrimination, Xenophobia and Related Intolerance: Declaration and Programme of Action, 2001.

Reference

Reitano R (1999) Summits, multilateral diplomacy, and the United Nations. In: Muldoon JP Jr et al (eds) Multilateral diplomacy and the United Nations today. Westview Press, Boulder

The Durban Conference and Its Impact on the Recognition of People of African Descent as Subjects of International Law

Pastor Elías Murillo Martínez

1 Introduction

The Durban Conference represents the most important milestone on the path to combating racism and racial discrimination at a global level, following the International Convention on the Elimination of All Forms of Racial Discrimination, adopted by the United Nations in 1965. Indeed, although two world conferences against racism had been held before (1978 and 1983), their focus was on combating the apartheid system, which for more than four decades imposed a white minority against the population including black and Indian in South Africa and Namibia. In the Durban process, racism was addressed from a global perspective.

In this sense, Durban had and continues to have positive impacts in the fight against racism, racial discrimination, xenophobia, and other related forms of intolerance that affect certain social groups. This has been a framework of reference for strengthening the legal, institutional, and instrumental architecture to combat racism and racial discrimination.

In the opinion of Daniel Achebron, who served as part of the UN Secretariat team, "the Durban Declaration and Programme of Action represents a step forward in the process of true universalization of the rights proclaimed in the Universal Declaration of Human Rights and the successive pacts. In this sense, the people who

---

Readers can access the Spanish version of this chapter through the electronic supplementary material provided.

Supplementary Information The online version contains supplementary material available at https://doi.org/10.1007/978-3-032-17265-5_7.

P. E. M. Martínez (✉)
United Nations Permanent Forum on People of African Descent, Bogotá, Colombia

C. S. Namakula (ed.), *Untold Reflections from the World Conference Against Racism*, SpringerBriefs in Law, https://doi.org/10.1007/978-3-032-17265-5_7

defeated colonialism became major protagonists of the [universal] purpose of international human rights law over years of political struggles and diplomatic processes. This is one of the achievements of the Durban Conference."[1]

From this perspective, this document focuses on the impact that the Durban Conference has had on people of African descent, which is of special importance for the full validity of human rights, international peace, and security, in the current context. Thus, the emergence of people of African descent as a subject of international law, considered in its broadest sense, is highlighted as one of the facts of special relevance in the analysis of the impact of the Durban Conference. As will be explained later, the concept of Afro-descendants was adopted in Durban, after the significant contribution made by the Regional Preparatory Conference of Santiago, Chile.

Afro-descendants represent nearly 300 million people, of which more than 200 million are located in the region of the Americas, that is, more than 20% of the total population of the continent. In South America, many Afro-descendant communities are settled in key areas for environmental sustainability, the energy transition, and the supply chain. Many of the main ports in the region are located in the ancestral territories of Afro-descendants and also the Panama Canal, through which around 6% of global trade moves.

Notwithstanding this important advance in the recognition of people of African descent, it is important to note that the opposition to the Durban Conference, displayed by Israel, had as its epilogue, the adoption of the Durban Declaration and Programme of Action (DDPA) without unanimous support and the blockade on its implementation, which persists, under the leadership of Israel with the support of some of its allies, especially the United States and the United Kingdom. The mere mention of Durban was banned in any document from those countries or involving them.

This opposition is due, first, to the tensions that arose around the issues of anti-Semitism and Islamophobia, which have the conflict between Israel and Palestine as a backdrop. Indeed, even before the Conference, the Jewish lobby deployed aggressive diplomatic action, which included unilateral coercive measures against some countries, to persuade them not to participate in the Durban Conference, under the argument that it was a hidden way of condemning Zionism and promoting anti-Semitism. Colombia, for example, was asked by the Jewish Caucus of the United States House of Representatives to desist from participating in the Conference, under penalty of consequences for its bilateral policy with the USA.

It must be pointed out that the bias argued by Israel is not reflected in the document adopted in Durban. On the contrary, "the Durban Declaration and Programme of Action reminds us that the Holocaust must never be forgotten."[2]

On the other hand, the terrorist attack on the Twin Towers in New York, which caused the death of nearly three thousand people, would also undermine the impacts of Durban. This event, which occurred on September 11, 2001, when barely 3 days

[1] Statement at the World Conference against Racism, 2001.

[2] Durban Declaration and Programme of Action, 2001, para 58.

had passed after the Durban Conference had concluded, eclipsed the human rights agenda, at the national and international levels, which was displaced by the fight against terrorism. There was a lost decade of setbacks in the field of human rights that marked the relativization of the human essence, which persists and expands throughout the twenty-first century.

This chapter addresses the emergence of people of African descent as a subject of international law by exploring the following respectively: (1) the aspects related to the process of the Preparatory Conference of Santiago de Chile; (2) people of African descent in the Durban Declaration and Programme of Action; (3) the influence of Durban on the path towards recognition, justice and development of people of African descent; and, finally, (4) the Afro-descendant Agenda for a second International Decade and an International Declaration on the Promotion, Protection and Full Respect of the Human Rights of People of African Descent, which is in progress under the auspices of the United Nations.

2 The Santiago Conference: The Gateway to International Recognition of People of African Descent

The Regional Conference in Santiago, Chile, was attended by 35 countries of the Americas in addition to the unconventional participation of the United States and Canada. It was preceded by the NGO Forum[3] held on December 2 and 3, 2000, also in Santiago, in which a large number of spokespersons for indigenous peoples came together, the Afro-descendant people, the Roma or Gypsy people, and their intersectionality, including migrants and the LGTBIQ+ community, among other social expressions.

In Santiago, the States adopted a Declaration and Plan of Action[4] by consensus that served as a central reference for their positions and even for the Durban Conference itself. It should be noted that this Conference gave centrality to the issue of people of African descent.

According to the Santiago +5 Pre-Conference Framework against Racism, Xenophobia, Discrimination, and Intolerance (2005), "the Santiago Declaration and Action Plan are advanced instruments for combating racism on the continent, and the current assessment reflects their great capacity to identify the origin, causes, and victims of racism. Afro-descendants, indigenous people, immigrants, women, disabled people, and children were recognized by the Conference as the main victims of racism and discrimination. (...) Likewise, the possibility of advancing the

[3] https://poblacionafroperuana.cultura.pe/sites/default/files/santiago_5_0.pdf.

[4] WCR/IC/2001/Misc.5. Accessed from https://www.oas.org/dil/2000%20Declaration%20of%20the%20Conference%20of%20the%20Americas%20(Preparatory%20meeting%20for%20the%20Third%20World%20Conference%20against%20Racism,%20Racial%20Discrimination,%20Xenophobia%20and%20Related%20Intolerance).pdf on 17 April 2025.

implementation of the right to reparations for the damage caused by slavery was accepted."[5]

For Afro-descendants, the Citizens' Conference (or NGO Forum), and the Regional Conference of Santiago de Chile, meant a fundamental shift on the path towards their recognition, justice, and development. Before Santiago and Durban, there was a lack of an internationally recognized concept to refer to the African diaspora, which, among other consequences, limited their recognition as victims of the Trans-Atlantic trade in enslaved people and its perpetuation through racism and racial discrimination. That situation restricted the inclusion of the issues of people of African descent on the international agenda. Durban filled that void.

The concept of Afro-descendants was coined, unanimously, at the aforementioned Regional Preparatory Conference of Santiago de Chile following a demand by the Social Movement of Afro-descendants. As Romero Rodríguez, one of its most emblematic leaders, stated: "We entered as blacks and left as Afro-descendants."[6]

According to the OAS and the Inter-American Commission on Human Rights, an Afro-descendant is described as "... a person of African origin who lives in the Americas and in all areas of the African diaspora as a consequence of slavery, having been historically denied the exercise of their fundamental rights".[7] A broader definition could consider people of African descent as those who self-identify as such; the children of victims of Trans-Atlantic trafficking; the descendants of contemporary migrations from Africa and the group of families of African descent that have their own culture, share a history, and have their traditions and customs that reveal and preserve awareness of identity that distinguishes them from other ethnic groups.

Notwithstanding the above, the description of an Afro-descendant is a matter that has not yet been settled. The process for the adoption of an International Declaration on the Promotion, Protection, and Full Respect of the Human Rights of People of African Descent, represents an exceptional opportunity to move towards a universally recognised definition.

---

[5] Bello (2005), p. 2.

[6] De La Fuente (2018). Available from: https://scholar.harvard.edu/files/kennedylorenzini/files/12-13-17_spreads_low_res.pdf.

[7] Organization of American States [OAS]; and Inter-American Commission on Human Rights [IACHR] (2011), p. 7, para 19: the term "Afro-descendants" was coined as a political and legal concept at the Regional Conference of the Americas in Santiago, Chile, preparatory to the Third World Conference against Racism, Racial Discrimination, Xenophobia and Related Forms of Intolerance, held in Durban (South Africa) in 2001.

3 People of African Descent in the Durban Declaration and Programme of Action

As already indicated, one of the most notable outcomes of the Durban Conference was the recognition of the Afro-descendant as a subject of international law and their condition as victim of racism and racial discrimination. Thus, the Durban Declaration and Programme of Action, hereinafter DDPA, recognizes the persistence of the legacy of enslavement among Africans and people of African descent as follows:

> We acknowledge that slavery and the slave trade, including the trans-Atlantic slave trade, were appalling tragedies in the history of humanity not only because of their abhorrent barbarism but also in terms of their magnitude, organized nature and especially their negation of the essence of the victims, and further acknowledge that slavery and the slave trade are a crime against humanity and should always have been so, especially the trans-Atlantic slave trade, and are among the major sources and manifestations of racism, racial discrimination, xenophobia and related intolerance, and that Africans and people of African descent, Asians and people of Asian descent and indigenous peoples were victims of these acts and continue to be victims of their consequences.[8]
>
> (...) We recognize that people of African descent have for centuries been victims of racism, racial discrimination and enslavement and of the denial by history of many of their rights, and assert that they should be treated with fairness and respect for their dignity and should not suffer discrimination of any kind. Recognition should therefore be given to their rights to culture and their own identity; to participate freely and in equal conditions in political, social, economic and cultural life; to development in the context of their own aspirations and customs; to keep, maintain and foster their own forms of organization, their mode of life, culture, traditions and religious expressions; to maintain and use their own languages; to the protection of their traditional knowledge and their cultural and artistic heritage; to the use, enjoyment and conservation of the natural renewable resources of their habitat and to active participation in the design, implementation and development of educational systems and programmes, including those of a specific and characteristic nature; and where applicable to their ancestrally inhabited land.[9]

The DDPA urges States and the United Nations, and calls on a wide range of organizations, to adopt concrete measures to eliminate the consequences and enduring legacies of enslavement. To contribute to this purpose, Durban envisaged the creation of a Working Group of experts on people of African descent,[10] which is complemented by the role of the Intergovernmental Working Group on the Effective Implementation of the Durban Declaration and Program of Action; the Group of Independent Eminent Experts on the Durban Declaration and Programme of Action and, more recently, with the Permanent Forum on People of African Descent and the "Expert Mechanism to Promote Racial Justice and Equality in Law Enforcement", known as the George Floyd Mechanism.

[8] DDPA, para 13.

[9] DDPA, para 34.

[10] DDPA, para 7.

Of note is the Committee on the Elimination of Racial Discrimination (CERD), which has stood out for its special role of follow up on Durban.[11] On the occasion of the examination of periodic reports, the CERD evaluates the compliance of States concerning the DDPA. The concluding observations include a standard paragraph with specific recommendations in this regard. At the request of CERD, the International Year for People of African Descent (2011) and the International Decade for People of African Descent, which originally occurred between the year 2015 and 2024, and was renewed for 2025 to 2034, were created. As noted in its report to the General Assembly CERD also recommended the adoption of an International Declaration on the Rights of People of African Descent,[12] which is in progress and has the DDPA as its main frame of reference. The holding of a World Conference on People of African Descent[13] is also part of the recommendations of the Committee.[14]

4 The Influence of Durban on the Path Toward Recognition, Justice, and Development of People of African Descent

The Declaration and Programme of Action adopted in Durban constitutes the framework of reference for the legal, institutional, and instrumental architecture to advance the path towards recognition, justice, and development of people of African descent. Indeed, a set of resolutions and decisions have been adopted within the framework of the United Nations that today constitute the legal corpus of the rights of people of African descent.

At the level of the United Nations, it is worth highlighting the General Assembly resolution proclaiming the International Year of People of African Descent.[15] This resolution was adopted upon overcoming the opposition of several regional groups to an initial draft resolution, presented by Colombia in 2009, which had the proclamation of an international decade for people of African descent as its objective. Some of the countries, particularly from the Western bloc, that expressed their opposition did so in rejection to the multiple references to Durban contained in the said draft resolution. Colombian diplomacy led to a compromise solution, which culminated into a text that, on the one hand, reduced expectations to one year and, on the other hand, incorporated only a mention of Durban in its recitals. This

[11] See for example, General Recommendation No. 33: Follow-up to the Durban Review Conference, CERD/C/GC/33, 29 September 2009.

[12] See Report of the Committee on the Elimination of Racial Discrimination, General Assembly 67th Session Supplement No 18 (A/67/18) para 2.

[13] https://documents.un.org/doc/undoc/gen/g12/428/72/pdf/g1242872.pdf.

[14] See Report of the Committee on the Elimination of Racial Discrimination, General Assembly 67th Session Annex VII (A/67/18) para 4. https://documents.un.org/doc/undoc/gen/g12/428/72/pdf/g1242872.pdf. Accessed 27 June 2025.

[15] A/RES/64/169 12 March 2010 para 1.

mention vindicated the Durban Declaration and Programme of Action. Even with that reference, Colombia managed to get the United States to join as a co-sponsoring country.

In 2013, the United Nations General Assembly proclaimed the International Decade for People of African Descent,[16] under the leadership of South Africa, which, on this occasion, claimed its role as a host country of the third World Conference against Racism before Colombia and others. Precisely, the Durban demand kept the draft resolution captive for several years. The controversy extended to the Programme of activities for the implementation of the international decade for people of African descent,[17] which has as its axis the Durban Declaration and Programme of Action.

In this framework, it is also worth highlighting CERD's General Recommendation No. 34 on racial discrimination against people of African descent,[18] which, among other undertakings, summarizes the individual and collective rights of people of African descent, including the following:

> (a) The right to property and to the use, conservation and protection of lands traditionally occupied by them and to natural resources in cases where their ways of life and culture are linked to their utilization of lands and resources; (b) The right to their cultural identity, to keep, maintain and foster their mode of life and forms of organization, culture, languages and religious expressions; (c) The right to the protection of their traditional knowledge and their cultural and artistic heritage; (d) The right to prior consultation with respect to decisions which may affect their rights, in accordance with international standards[19]

At the regional level, the Organization of American States (OAS), the European Union (EU), and the African Union (AU) have also adopted resolutions and decisions relating to people of African descent. International resolutions and decisions feed back into the processes of legal recognition of Afro-descendants at national levels, particularly in the South American region.

In the region of the Americas, it is worth highlighting the Inter-American Convention against Racism, Racial Discrimination, and Related Forms of Intolerance,[20] adopted in 2013, under the leadership of Brazil. It was originally a single Convention, but in the end and as a compromise solution, it was divided into two instruments to overcome the controversies that threatened to frustrate the entire process due to differences related to certain intersectionalities, including gender and religion, particularly from the countries of the Community of Latin American and Caribbean States (CARICOM).

With regard specifically to people of African descent, at the hemispheric level, it is worth highlighting the Plan of Action for the Decade of People of African Descent

---

[16] A/RES/68/237 07 February 2014.

[17] https://docs.un.org/en/A/RES/69/16. Accessed 27 June 2025.

[18] CERD/C/GC/34 03 March 2011.

[19] Ibid para 4.

[20] Antigua, 05 June 2013, entered into force on 11 November 2017. Accessed from https://treaties.un.org/doc/Publication/UNTS/No%20Volume/54915/Part/I-54915-08000002804ec1cd.pdf on 19 April 2025.

in the Americas (2016–2025)[21,22] adopted by the General Assembly of the Organization of American States (OAS),[23] and the resolution on the Inter-American Week for People of African Descent in the Americas on February 21, 2018, approved by the Permanent Council of the OAS.[24] Also worth highlighting is, the Inter-American Commission on Human Rights, among others. The Commission established a rapporteurship on the rights of persons of African descent and against racial discrimination in 2005, which works with OAS member states to (1) raise awareness of the states' duty to respect the human rights of Afro-descendants and on the elimination of all forms of discrimination; (2) analyse the challenges encountered by countries in these areas; (3) formulate recommendations designed to overcome obstacles; (4) identify and share best practices in the region with respect to this matter; and (5) provide technical assistance requested by member states in the implementation of the recommendations in national law and practice.[25] The IACHR has also made bold pronouncements on police brutality,[26] the obligation of the state to ensure effective remedies for victims of racial discrimination,[27] racism in the criminal justice system in the Americas,[28] and racial inequality in participation in government.[29]

Increasingly, both the Inter-American Commission and the Inter-American Court of Human Rights have begun to address the issue of racism and racial discrimination with greater emphasis, granting growing recognition to the rights of Afro-descendants within the Inter-American System. This evolution is reflected in the strengthening of the recognition of Afro-descendants as collective subjects of rights and, in some cases, as peoples with differentiated rights—particularly regarding their ancestral territories, cultural identity, and autonomy.

One of the most emblematic cases in this process is *Saramaka People v. Suriname*[30] in which the Inter-American Court recognized the Afro-descendant

---

[21] https://www.oas.org/en/sare/documents/res-2891-16-en.pdf.

[22] AG/RES 2891(XLVI-O/16). Accessed from https://www.oas.org/en/sare/documents/res-2891-16-en.pdf on 21 April 2025.

[23] OAS, AG/RES. 2891 (XLVI-O/16).

[24] OAS, CP/RES. 1093 (2144/18). https://www.oas.org/en/media_center/press_release.asp?sCodigo=S-004/18.

[25] Accessed from https://www.oas.org/en/IACHR/jsForm/?File=/en/IACHR/R/DPAD/Default.asp on 21 April 2025.

[26] Wallace De Almeida, Admissibility and Merits, Brazil, Case 12.440, 20 March 2009, Report No 26/09 paras 141,149, and 150. Accessed from https://cidh.oas.org//annualrep/2009eng/Brazil12440eng.htm on 22 April 2025.

[27] Simone André Diniz, Merits, Case 12.001, 21 October 2006, para 146, Report No 66/06. Accessed from https://cidh.oas.org/annualrep/2006eng/BRAZIL.12001eng.htm on 22 April 2025.

[28] Kevin Cooper, Merits, Case 12.831, 28 October 2015, Report No 78/15, paras 138 – 140. Accessed from https://www.oas.org/en/iachr/decisions/2015/USPU12831EN.pdf on 22 April 2025.

[29] Statehood Solidarity Committee, Case 11.204, Report No 98/03, para 98. Accessed from https://cidh.org/annualrep/2003eng/USA.11204a.htm on 22 April 2025.

[30] Judgment, Inter-Am. Ct. H.R. (ser. C) No. 172, (Nov. 28, 2007). Available from: https://www.corteidh.or.cr/docs/casos/articulos/seriec_172_ing.pdf.

Saramaka community as a tribal people with collective rights over their ancestral lands. This judgment marked a milestone by establishing standards on free, prior, and informed consent and on the effective participation in decisions affecting their territories, further developing the regional scope of ILO Convention 169 and setting a key precedent for the protection of territorial rights of Afro-descendants.[31]

In the case of *Acosta Martínez et al. v. Argentina*,[32] the Inter-American Court addressed the illegal, arbitrary, and discriminatory detention of José Delfín Acosta Martínez, an Afro-descendant Uruguayan citizen. Acosta Martínez was detained by the Argentine police on charges of public intoxication. During his detention, Acosta Martínez was subjected to mistreatment and subsequently died while in police custody. The Court found that the detention was illegal, arbitrary, and motivated by racial discrimination.[33]

In parallel to these jurisprudential advances, significant institutional developments have taken place within the framework of the Organization of American States (OAS), such as the creation of the Inter-American Network of High Authorities on Policies for Afro-descendant Populations (RIAFRO), which promotes technical cooperation and the exchange of best practices for the design and implementation of public policies with an ethnic-racial approach.[34] Currently, the OAS is advancing the development of an Inter-American Declaration on the Rights of Afro-descendant Persons, an instrument aimed at consolidating a regional normative framework for the recognition, reparation, and guarantee of their rights across the continent. This process was formally initiated through Resolution AG/RES. 3028 (LIV-O/24)[35] of the OAS General Assembly, which established the creation of a working group tasked with drafting the declaration.[36]

The European Parliament adopted a resolution on Fundamental Rights of People of African Descent in Europe.[37] The resolution confirms the various identity formations of people of African ancestry born in Europe, are citizens or that live in Europe as 'Afro-European', 'African European', 'Black European', 'Afro-Caribbean', or 'Black Caribbean'.[38] It also recognises anti-black racism as a specific form of racism

[31] Saramaka People v. Suriname, Preliminary Objections, Merits, Reparations, and Costs, Case Series C No. 172, November 28, 2007. Accessed from https://www.corteidh.or.cr/docs/casos/articulos/seriec_172_ing.pdf on 29 April 2025.

[32] Judgment, August 31, 2020. (Merits, reparations and costs). Available from: https://www.corteidh.or.cr/docs/casos/articulos/seriec_410_ing.pdf.

[33] Acosta Martínez et al. v. Argentina, Merits, reparations and costs, Case Series C No. 410, August 31, 2020. Accessed from https://www.corteidh.or.cr/docs/casos/articulos/seriec_410_ing.pdf on 29 April 2025.

[34] https://www.oas.org/ext/en/human-rights/riafro#:~:text=The%20RIAFRO%20was%20created%20in,of%20civil%20society%20and%20organizations. Accessed 29 April 2025.

[35] https://www.refworld.org/es/leg/resol/oea/2024/es/149207.

[36] Resolution AG/RES. 3028 (LIV-O/24). https://www.refworld.org/es/leg/resol/oea/2024/es/149207. Accessed 29 April 2025.

[37] European Parliament resolution of 26 March 2019 on fundamental rights of people of African descent in Europe (2018/2899 (RSP).

[38] Ibid para A.

fuelled by historical abuses and negative stereotyping, and leading to the exclusion and dehumanization of people of African descent.[39] The resolution is also explicit about the nature of racism experienced by people of African descent as structural and often intersectional,[40] while correlating to historically repressive structures of colonialism and the trans-Atlantic slave trade.[41]

There are also inter-continental collaborative efforts such as the engagement between the African Union and the Americas on matters concerning the African diaspora including the issue of reparations for enslavement of Africans and people of African descent.[42] The resolution of the European Parliament itself encourages interaction with international actors to combat Afrophobia at the international level.[43]

In summary, the Durban Conference was the landmark event that propelled the emergence of issues of people of African descent and the main developments concerning them in the international sphere. The DDPA per se constitutes a framework for action, among other instruments.

Finally, it is worth highlighting that the Durban Declaration and Programme of Action have also served as support for South American countries to adopt new legal frameworks aimed at combating racism and racial discrimination. In that sense, more than two decades after Durban, it is noted that the region has experienced significant progress on the path toward recognition, justice, and development of people of African descent.

First, the 20 countries in the region have incorporated the ethnic-racial variable in their national censuses and are making progress in administrative records, which has resulted in greater visibility. Thus, for example, today it is known that Afro-descendants are 56% of the population in Brazil, that is, more than 110 million people, who, together with the 50 million people in the United States represent around 80% of the total of Afro-descendants in the region, followed by Colombia, where nearly 5 million have identified themselves as such, although empirical data places their number at more than 10 million people.

Second, some countries such as Brazil, Colombia, Ecuador, Uruguay, Bolivia, and Costa Rica have adopted quotas for affirmative action measures concerning access to public office and higher education. In Brazil, for example, until a decade ago, Afro-descendants were barely 10% of students in public universities; they are around 55% today following allocation of quotas. In Brazil and Colombia, there is a growing critical mass of Afro-descendants that have undertaken postgraduate studies in international universities as a result of affirmative action measures, which is positively impacting the political representation and quality of employment of Afro-descendants in those countries.

---

[39] Ibid para B.

[40] Ibid para S.

[41] Ibid para B.

[42] See Declaration of the Global African Diaspora Summit, Diaspora/Assembly/AU/Decl(I), Sandton, Johannesburg, South Africa, 25 May 2012.

[43] European Parliament resolution of 26 March 2019, para 27.

Third, in terms of political representation in the last decade, two women, Epsy Campbell Barr and Francia Márquez became vice presidents of Costa Rica and Colombia respectively; in Ecuador, Diana Salazar is the Attorney General of the nation; in Colombia, an Afro-descendant, Gerson Chaverra, presides over the Supreme Court of Justice for the first time in history, while in Costa Rica, the activist Angie Cruickshank Lambert was elected Ombudsperson, the first in the region. Likewise, the access of Afro-descendants, especially women, to ministerial positions and diplomatic representations in various countries, mainly in Africa, is increasingly common, with Colombia being the most emblematic case.

However, political representation of people of African descent in Brazil is less than 10%. Of the 66 members of the Federal Senate, only fifteen are women and of these, only one is of African descent; Of the 1,280 people who make up Brazil's diplomatic corps, only 189 are of African descent and only four have the rank of ambassador, out of a total of 175. Following the approval of the Plurinational Plan for the Elimination of Racial Discrimination,[44] the government of Ecuador incorporated a contingent of indigenous, Afro-descendant, and Montubios into its diplomatic ranks. Meanwhile, in Colombia, the presence of Afro-descendants in the diplomatic career is minimal. Only one career official has just obtained the rank of Ambassador.

Regarding territorial and land policies in Brazil, Colombia, Ecuador, Honduras and Suriname, around 9 million hectares of land have been awarded to Afro-descendants as collective property of their ancestral territories, of which nearly 6 million are located in Colombia, which has commenced a kind of peaceful agrarian revolution.

From another perspective, the path toward restorative justice for people of African descent also began to be paved in Durban. Among the voices that resonated most strongly is that of the Secretary General of the United Nations himself, Kofi Annan, who emphasized the urgent need to acknowledge and address the enduring legacies of slavery and the trans-Atlantic slave trade and that despite the formal abolition of slavery more than two centuries ago, its consequences remain evident in the social and economic inequalities affecting Afro-descendant communities around the world. He underscored the importance of confronting these historical injustices through public policies that promote equity and inclusion.[45] The then president of Cuba, Fidel Castro, spoke in the same direction, raising his voice to echo the demands for historical reparation, raised by the countries of South America at the Regional Preparatory Conference in Santiago.

There are many milestones to highlight, in terms of historical reparation, that are part of the impact of the Durban Conference: (1) Pope John Paul II apologized for

---

[44] Executive Decree No. 60 (28 September 2009).

[45] https://www.unodc.org/unodc/en/about-unodc/speeches/speech_2007_05_08.html#:~:text=In%20short%2C%20ladies%20and%20gentlemen,of%20slaves%20is%20obvious%20enough. Accessed 20 June 2025.

the trans-Atlantic slave trade and enslavement,[46] and later, in 1992, during a visit to Gorée Island, he issued an apology on behalf of Europe and denounced the clerics who had blessed the slave ships;[47] (2) the recognition of trans-Atlantic trafficking and slavery as a crime against humanity, by the French Parliament;[48] (3) Germany's recognition of colonial genocide against the Nama and Herero of Namibia, including its provision of financial reparation; (4) the collapse of statues and other symbols of slave traders and notaries in the United States (Manchester), and later in Europe and South America; the replacement of names of slaveholders on street names in European States (Belgium, France, Switzerland and the United Kingdom); (5) reparations paid by AETNA insurance to Caribbean countries and the recent request for forgiveness from the King of the Netherlands, among others.

5 The Afro-Descendant Agenda: Deepening the Recognition, Justice and Development of Afro-Descendants

In Durban, the States recognized the reality of systemic and structural racism against people of African descent. "Systemic racism against Africans and people of African descent, that includes structural and institutional racism, is understood as the operation of a complex and interrelated system of laws, policies, practices and attitudes in institutions, the State, the private sector and social structures that, combined, give rise to discrimination, distinction, exclusion, restriction or preference, direct or indirect, intentional or unintentional, in fact or law, based on race, color, ancestry or national or ethnic origin".[49] "Systemic racism frequently manifests itself in the form of widespread racial stereotypes, racial profiling, prejudices, and biases, and is rooted in the histories and legacies of slavery, the trans-Atlantic African slave trade, and colonialism."[50]

Despite the advances in human rights mentioned above, various analyses confirm the persistence of systemic racism that Afro-descendants experience. Among these studies is the report of the Commission on Social Determinants of Health, titled "Just Societies: Equity in Health and a Dignified Life",[51] which sets out the following:

---

[46] https://www.nytimes.com/1985/08/14/world/pope-apologizes-to-africans-for-slavery.html. Accessed 29 April 2025.

[47] Accessed from https://africarenewal.un.org/en/magazine/goree-island-and-fragility-freedom on 29 April 2025.

[48] Law of May 21, 2001 (Taubira).

[49] "Promotion and Protection of the Human Rights and Fundamental Freedoms of Africans and of People of African Descent against Excessive Use of Force and Other Human Rights Violations by Law Enforcement Officers", A/HRC/47/53, 01 June 2021, para 9.

[50] A/HRC/47/53. UN, 2021.

[51] https://iris.paho.org/handle/10665.2/51615. Accessed 27 June 2025.

5.1 Poverty

In Latin America, Afro-descendants make up 50% of the population living in poverty, even though they constitute only 1/4 of the total population. The risks of poverty are cumulative,[52] on average, the income of Afro-descendant women reached just 51% of the income of Afro-descendant men in 2014.

In the United States of America, 19% of older African Americans and 18% of older Hispanic people live in poverty, compared to 9% of older white people. In Colombia, the effect of ethnic-racial status on poverty was confirmed. Given the same characteristics of the people, being of African descent increases the probability of being poor by 75% and the probability of being in extreme poverty by 140%.

5.2 Education

Afro-descendants register large gaps in access to education, including higher education, which affects the quality of employment, health, and justice, among others. A 2022 World Bank report[53] on Afro-descendant Inclusion in Education states that "in Latin America, there are 34 million Afro-descendants of school age. However, statistics indicate that 7 million of them will leave the educational system before finishing primary school, double the regional average compared to their non-Afro-descendant peers.[54] Representations in school books often do not promote recognition of the identity of Afro-descendant communities and, on the contrary, contribute to promoting folkloric representations and stereotypes".[55] The World Bank study includes a review of 5,121 images from 40 primary and secondary school books from 10 Latin American countries. In them, Afro-descendant people were only represented in 15% of the images, mostly in activities associated with music, sports, rural, manual, or industrial work.

The report notes that "while Latin America is experiencing a widespread learning crisis, Afro-descendant students are among the most affected.[56] In Brazil, for example, almost half of black children could not read or understand age-appropriate text, compared to 39% of non-black children. In Colombia, the situation is just as

[52] Freire et al. (2022).

[53] https://documents1.worldbank.org/curated/en/099056005022316092/pdf/IDU05497146208ea8042190919d0d27079d7a405.pdf.

[54] See Why would seven million Afro-descendant children drop out of elementary school? World Bank Group, 28 May 2023. https://www.worldbank.org/en/news/feature/2023/05/28/why-would-7-million-afro-descendant-children-drop-out-of-elementary-school.

[55] Note 47 above.

[56] Ibid.

worrying, "almost 7 in 10 Black children were unable to understand age-appropriate text in 2019, compared to about 4 in 10 of their non-Black peers."[57]

The deficient situation of education among people of African descent, added to racism and racial discrimination, has a drastic impact on their employability and tends to worsen due to the disruptive impacts of artificial intelligence and automation, which negatively affect them. Of note is the differentiated manner by multiple factors including the digital divide. Indeed, in Colombia, for example, the average connectivity coverage for Afro-descendants is 45%; it does not reach 50%.

5.3 Child Mortality

Between 2003 and 2017, mortality in children under 1 year of age fell by 42% in Latin America and the Caribbean and it remained below 10 per 1000 in the United States and 5 per 1000 in Canada. In seven of the eight Latin American countries for which there is data, mortality in children under 1 year of age was higher in 2010 in children of African descent than in other children.

5.4 Child Labor

The Americas region has the third largest burden of child labor in the world. In 2017, there were 10.7 million children and adolescents between 5 and 17 years old in the labor market. In 2014 in Brazil, around 60% of working children aged 5–13 were of African descent.

5.5 Maternal Health and Postnatal Care

Large differences persist in the maternal mortality rate between countries, ranging from 4.8 deaths of women in childbirth per 100,000 live births in Canada to more than 220 per 100,000 live births in Guyana and Haiti.

In Costa Rica, 87% of Afro-descendant women received prenatal care in 2013, compared to 92% of women from other groups. In Uruguay, 78% of Afro-descendant women received prenatal care in 2011, compared to 90% of non-Afro-descendant women. It should be noted that the region neither achieved Millennium Development Goal 5 of reducing the maternal mortality rate by 75% between 1990 and 2015 nor universal access to reproductive health services by 2015.

[57] Ibid.

5.6 *Life Expectancy*

The life expectancy of Afro-descendants is noticeably lower than the national averages and the gap widens in areas of increased population density. In the city of Baltimore, United States, in 2014, there was a 19-year disparity in life expectancy between the most disadvantaged and the most affluent neighborhoods.[58] While a woman in Haiti has a life expectancy of just under 66 years, it is 84 years in Canada.

5.7 *Violence*

Latin America and the Caribbean have the highest homicide rates in the world, which in 2015 was 22 per 100,000 inhabitants, while the second highest rate, recorded in sub-Saharan Africa, was 9 per 100,000.[59] Violence against Afro-descendants in the United States is widely known; the country registers high rates of homicides against this population, which is associated with the practice of racial profiling. After the murder of George Floyd, the United Nations created the Independent Expert Mechanism to Promote Racial Justice and Equality in the Application of the Law (EMLER). Its reports document the seriousness of this phenomenon and the contexts in which it occurs.[60]

The evidence reveals a persistent and well-documented pattern of disproportionate incarceration affecting people of African descent in the United States. Although Black Americans represent only around 13% of the U.S. population, they account for approximately 38% of the federal prison population.[61] Moreover, they are incarcerated at a rate six times higher than white individuals, even in states considered progressive.[62] Overall, nearly two million people are held in prisons and jails across the country, with Black individuals significantly overrepresented among them—reflecting the systemic racial disparities that characterize the U.S. criminal legal system.[63] In Colombia, the disproportionate impacts of the internal armed conflict on Afro-descendants are also known, coupled with cases associated with racial profiling.

[58] https://iris.paho.org/handle/10665.2/51615, p. 148. Accessed 15 July 2025.

[59] Ibid p. 177.

[60] A/HRC/54/69 https://docs.un.org/en/A/HRC/54/69. Available from: https://www.ohchr.org/es/documents/thematic-reports/ahrc5469-promotion-and-protection-human-rights-and-fundamental-freedoms.

[61] https://www.americanprogress.org/article/8-facts-you-should-know-about-the-criminal-justice-system-and-people-of-color/#:~:text=People%20of%20color%20are%20significantly,of%20those%20who%20are%20incarcerated and https://www.bop.gov/about/statistics/statistics_inmate_race.jsp. Accessed 15 July 2025.

[62] https://static.prisonpolicy.org/reports/PPI_Annual_2023-2024.pdf. Accessed 14 July 2025.

[63] https://www.sentencingproject.org/reports/mass-incarceration-trends/. Accessed 14 July 2025.

The murder of Council woman Marielle Franco in Rio de Janeiro in 2018 marked a turning point in the invisibility of violence against people of African descent in Brazil. State-sanctioned violence in Brazil is both persistent and highly racialized, disproportionately affecting people of African descent. In 2022 alone, police forces in eight Brazilian states were responsible for 4,219 deaths. Of these, 2700 victims, approximately 65.7%, were identified as Black or mixed race.[64] When considering only the cases in which racial data was provided (3171 in total), the proportion of Black victims rises to 87.4%.[65] The state of Bahia stood out as the most lethal, with 1,465 people killed by its military police. Of the 1,183 victims whose racial data was available, 1,121 were Black, equivalent to 94.8%, a percentage significantly higher than the share of Black people in the state's general population (80.8%).[66]

The scale and frequency of this violence are staggering. An Afro-descendant person was killed by the police every 4 hours in Brazil in 2022.[67] UN experts from the International Independent Expert Mechanism to Advance Racial Justice and Equality in Law Enforcement, after a country visit in 2023, described these incidents as part of an alarming pattern rather than isolated events.[68] They emphasized how systemic police brutality has led to a deep erosion of trust between law enforcement and marginalized communities.[69] Each year, more than 6,000 people are killed by police in Brazil, and Black individuals are three times more likely to be victims than white individuals.[70]

In 2023, this racialized dynamic of state violence persisted. According to the *Rede de Observatórios da Segurança*, police were responsible for 4,025 deaths across Brazil. Of the 3,169 victims whose racial data were available, 2,782 were Black Brazilians, representing 87.8% of the total. In all nine states analyzed, Black people were overwhelmingly overrepresented among victims of police killings: from 66.3% in São Paulo to 95.7% in Pernambuco. Bahia once again registered the highest number of killings (1,702), marking a 161% increase in deaths by police intervention compared to 2019. The report highlights the institutional reinforcement of racial stereotypes within police forces, where Black youth from favelas and

---

[64] https://www.brasildefato.com.br/2023/11/21/in-2022-65-out-of-every-100-people-killed-by-the-police-in-brazil-are-black-a-study-found/. Accessed 14 July 2025.

[65] Ibid.

[66] Ibid.

[67] https://www.dw.com/es/brasil-un-afrodescendiente-muerto-cada-4-horas-por-polic%C3%ADas/a-67448264. Accessed 14 July 2025.

[68] https://www.ohchr.org/en/documents/country-reports/ahrc5771add1-international-independent-expert-mechanism-advance-racial, and https://www.hrw.org/news/2024/10/10/un-experts-spotlight-devastating-police-brutality-brazil. Accessed 14 July 2025.

[69] Ibid.

[70] https://www.hrw.org/news/2024/10/10/un-experts-spotlight-devastating-police-brutality-brazil. Note 63 above.

peripheral areas are routinely perceived as suspects and treated as legitimate targets of state violence.[71]

Data published in 2025 confirm that the racialized pattern of police lethality observed in previous years remained consistent throughout 2024 and continued into 2025. According to the Anuário Brasileiro de Segurança Pública 2025, police actions resulted in 6,243 deaths across Brazil in 2024, representing approximately 14% of all violent deaths recorded in the country, disproportionately affecting Black and Afro-descendant populations (*Fórum Brasileiro de Segurança Pública*, 2025). Additionally, the report *Pele Alvo: crônicas de dor e luta* documents that in the nine states monitored by the *Rede de Observatórios da Segurança*, 4,068 deaths resulted from police interventions in 2024, of which 86.2% were Black individuals in cases where racial information was available (Ramos et al., 2025). This pattern of structural violence was also evident in 2025, when a bloody police operation in the Sierra da Misericórdia favela in Rio de Janeiro resulted in multiple deaths and injuries, highlighting the ongoing selective violence against vulnerable, predominantly Afro-descendant communities (El País, 2025). These findings demonstrate that police violence against Black populations in Brazil is not episodic, but structurally embedded in public security practices, reproducing persistent racial inequalities in the exercise of the State's coercive power (*Fórum Brasileiro de Segurança Pública*, 2025; Ramos et al., 2025; El País, 2025).

Police violence against people of African descent is also seen in Europe. In France, for example, "in 2021, 84.1% of the victims of police lethality were black, the majority young boys and children".[72] The European Union Agency for Fundamental Rights (FRA) highlights the resurgence of racism and racial discrimination and its disproportionate effects on Afro-descendants.[73] There is also a notable rise in far-right extremist groups in Europe. The main axis of the political discourse of such groups is xenophobia, the rejection of foreigners, mainly of African origin. In their narrative, they usually appeal, in an open or hidden way, to the theory of demographic reconversion or replacement. According to this theory, which is also invoked by the extreme right in the United States, large-scale migration to Europe and the United States is the product of a conspiracy aimed at "diluting the white race." Donald Trump eloquently interpreted this theory recently, stating immigrants are "poisoning the blood of our country."[74]

The theory of demographic reconversion or replacement ignores the deep causes of migration, including the deepening inequalities and climate change, exacerbated

---

[71] https://agenciabrasil.ebc.com.br/es/direitos-humanos/noticia/2024-11/brasilenos-muertos-por-la-policia-en-2023-casi-el-90-negros#:~:text=Un%20estudio%20publicado%20el%20jueves,representa%20el%2087%2C8%25. Accessed 14 July 2025.

[72] A/HRC/54/69 of 2023.

[73] Racism against People of African Descent is on the Rise in EU, European Union Agency for Fundamental Rights, the press release . 25 October 2023. Accessed 28 June 2025.

[74] https://www.cbsnews.com/news/trump-immigrants-poisoning-the-blood-of-our-country-reaction/, https://www.telegraph.co.uk/world-news/2023/10/06/donald-trump-far-right-immigrants-poison-blood-us/. Accessed 15 July 2025.

by the impacts of the fourth revolution, the digital divide marked by the use of artificial intelligence and automation tools, which disproportionately affect people of African descent.[75]

The report from the European Agency for Fundamental Rights (FRA) states that although, there has been binding legislation against discrimination in the EU since the year 2000 and important advances in policies since then, people of African descent continue to suffer racism, discrimination, and hate crimes.[76] "Almost half of people of African descent surveyed experience racial discrimination, an increase from 39 % in 2016 to 45 % in 2022.".[77] According to a new survey by the European Union Agency for Fundamental Human Rights, racist harassment and ethnic/racial profiling especially affecting young people, are common. The FRA calls on EU countries to take urgent action to address racial discrimination and harassment, to ensure that everyone is treated equally and with dignity.[78]

Some data contained in the report of the FRA illustrates the panorama of racism and racial discrimination against people of African descent in Europe:

Racial Discrimination 45% of respondents report having experienced racial discrimination in the 5 years before the survey, an increase from 39% in the previous FRA survey. In Germany and Austria, this percentage exceeds 70% of those surveyed. In most cases, they suffer discrimination when looking for work or housing. Young people and people with higher education are the most affected. However, discrimination remains invisible, with only 9% reporting it.

Harassment 30% of respondents say they have suffered racist harassment, but almost no one reports it. Young women, people with higher education, and those who wear religious clothing are more likely to experience racial harassment.

Police Checks Involving Racial Profiling 58% say that the last police check they were subjected to in the year before the survey used racial profiling. People who perceive that the policing they were subjected to used racial profiling trust the police much less.

Work 34% felt racially discriminated against during their job search and 31% at work in the 5 years before the survey. Compared to the general population, they are more likely to only have temporary contracts and to be overqualified for their jobs.

---

[75] A/77/549 of 2022. https://elpais.com/us/2025-07-12/una-jueza-prohibe-al-gobierno-de-trump-arrestar-a-migrantes-en-california-por-su-color-de-piel.html. Accessed 15 July 2025.

[76] European Agency for Fundamental Rights. Being black in the EU: experiences of people of African descent. 2024. https://fra.europa.eu/sites/default/files/fra_uploads/fra-2023-being-black_in_the_eu_en.pdf. Accessed 15 July 2025.

[77] https://fra.europa.eu/sites/default/files/fra_uploads/fra-2023-being-black_in_the_eu_en.pdf, p. 14. Accessed 15 July 2025.

[78] Ibid.

Housing and Poverty the increase in inflation and the cost of living has led a greater number of people of African descent to a situation of greater risk of poverty compared to the general population. Around 33% struggle to make ends meet and 14% cannot afford to keep their home warm, compared to 18% and 7% of the general population. Simply looking for accommodation is painful for many people, with 31% saying they have experienced racial discrimination when trying to find housing.

Education Young people of African descent are three times more likely to leave school prematurely than young people in general. More parents in 2022 say their children experienced racism at school than in 2016.

Given this panorama of systemic racism experienced by Afro-descendants, sustained and long-term efforts are required for its eradication, which justifies two important issues on the International Afro-Descendants' Agenda, such as the advancement of a second decade in favor of Afro-descendants and the adoption of an International Declaration on the Promotion, Protection and Full Respect of the Human Rights of People of African Descent, which, as already indicated, is in progress.

The Second Decade and the Declaration are key contributors to deepening the recognition, justice, and development of people of African descent, in a context of great challenges for international peace and security, many of which are associated with the political instrumentalization of racism and xenophobia, against certain social groups, of which Africans and Afro-descendants are among the main victims.

6 The Second International Decade: Towards a Third Generation of Rights for People of African Descent

The Second International Decade for People of African Descent (2025–2034), proclaimed by the United Nations General Assembly through Resolution 79/193 of December 2024,[79] and particularly the process aimed at formulating the corresponding programme of activities,[80] constitutes a timely opportunity to deepen efforts towards the consolidation of the Third Generation of Rights of People of African Descent.

The path towards racial equity for people of African descent is part of the third generation of rights. At first, Afro-descendants fought for freedom, which materialized in abolitionist laws, for the most part, in the mid-nineteenth century, with Brazil being the last country to abolish slavery, in 1888. A second generation of rights emerged in South America in the 1990s, after the end of the dictatorships and the

[79] https://docs.un.org/en/A/RES/79/193.

[80] https://www.ohchr.org/en/calls-for-input/2025/call-inputs-2025-report-united-nations-secretary-general-implementation.

emergence of constitutionalism of diversity, which questioned the myth of racial democracy. It focused on the demands of equality and non-discrimination and began to make way for the recognition of people of African descent as a collective subject of law at the national and international levels, which, among other areas, is expressed in the legal frameworks of ethnic recognition. Likewise, public policies with a differential approach and affirmative action measures have had great centrality.

In North America, although the abolition of slavery occurred in 1863, it was not until the 1960s and after the struggles of the civil rights movement that the path to racial equity commenced, and is still a long way off.

A third generation of rights for people of African descent is emerging. It transcends anti-racist struggles and focuses on reparation for the damage caused by trafficking, enslavement, and the prolongation of its consequences. This generation of rights also includes the right to climate justice and what can be called the right to digital equality including prevention and combating algorithmic bias.

Through the prism of reparations as a central theme of the third generation of rights, the path towards recognition, justice, and development of people of African descent requires observing the historical perspective of the struggles for freedom and equality of people of African descent, as the foundation on which the contemporary aspirational goals of Africans and people of African descent are built.

In this sense, states have adopted a second International Decade for People of African Descent, harnessing the results and achievements that have represented the frameworks for action in favor of people of African descent in recent years, mainly (a) the International Year for People of African Descent (2011), (b) the International Decade for People of African Descent (2015–2024) and (c) their respective programs of activities under the themes of recognition, justice, and development, based on the Durban Declaration and Programme of Action. The final evaluation report of the Decade, which will be presented by the Secretary of the United Nations General Assembly, will report on the progress and obstacles in achieving its objectives.[81]

7 Towards an "International Declaration on Respect, Protection and Realization of the Human Rights of People of African Descent"

The United Nations is advancing the discussion and drafting of an International Declaration on the Promotion, Protection, and Full Respect of the Human Rights of People of African Descent. From the perspective of the agency of the Afro-Descendant Social Movement, the declaration in progress has its roots in the

[81] "Programme of Activities for the Implementation of the International Decade for People of African Descent". A/79/290. 06 August 2024. Available from: https://docs.un.org/en/A/79/290. Accessed 07 July 2025.

Declaration on the Rights of the Black Peoples of the World,[82] led by Marcus Garvey and adopted in New York, in 1920, in a forum that included the participation of more than 10,000 people. At the request of the United Nations General Assembly in 2012,[83] the Committee on the Elimination of Racial Discrimination decided to "propose the preparation of a declaration on the promotion and full respect of the human rights of people of African descent."[84] The formulation of the draft Declaration is contemplated in resolution A/RES/76/226 of 2021 of the UN General Assembly[85] as follows:

> ...recalls the programme of activities for the International Decade for People of African Descent, in which it was recommended that a forum on people of African descent be established and that consideration be given to the elaboration of a draft United Nations declaration on the promotion and full respect of the human rights of people of African descent;
>
> (...) Requests the Intergovernmental Working Group on the Effective Implementation of the Durban Declaration and Programme of Action to devote at least half of its annual session to the elaboration of a draft United Nations declaration on the promotion and full respect of the human rights of people of African descent;
>
> (...) Invites the Permanent Forum of People of African Descent and the Working Group of experts on people of African descent, in accordance with their respective mandates, to contribute to the elaboration of a draft United Nations declaration on the promotion and full respect of the human rights of people of African descent.[86]

Thus, in compliance with the mandate of the United Nations General Assembly and after consultations with the different regional groups, the presidency of the Inter-Governmental Working Group (IGWG) was put forward for consideration as the leadership of the drafting process, which included the initial contributions of the Permanent Forum on People of African Descent and other interested parties. After several sessions in which substantial progress was made, surprisingly, the states requested a focus on the Durban language.[87]

The anticipated UN Declaration would be the first instrument to recognize people of African descent as a subject of international law, which entails their status as

---

[82] https://biblioteca-repositorio.clacso.edu.ar/bitstream/CLACSO/248378/1/Derechos-afrodescendientes.pdf.

[83] Report of the Committee on Racial Discrimination, A/67/18, 80th Session, 13 February – 09 March 2012. Annex VII, para. 2. https://documents.un.org/doc/undoc/gen/g12/428/72/pdf/g1242872.pdf.

[84] (CERD A/67/18). Available from: https://www2.ohchr.org/english/bodies/cerd/docs/A.67.18%20English.pdf.

[85] https://docs.un.org/en/A/RES/76/226.

[86] "A global call for concrete action for the elimination of racism, racial discrimination, xenophobia and related intolerance and the comprehensive implementation of and follow-up to the Durban Declaration and Programme of Action" A/RES/76/226, 10 January 2022, paras 9, 10, 11.

[87] See "Chairperson's document compiling existing human rights language on issues pertaining to the draft United Nations declaration on the respect, protection and fulfilment of the human rights of people of African descent", p. 1. https://www.ohchr.org/es/events/events/2024/22nd-session-intergovernmental-working-group-effective-implementation-durban. Accessed 07 July 2025.

a people. It would stipulate their national and international rights, and it has the potential to transcend into a binding instrument, as has been anticipated by the UN General Assembly itself. The most relevant precedent is General Recommendation 34 on Racism and Racial Discrimination against People of African Descent,[88] which summarizes some of their human rights standards, including their collective rights.

The Declaration would also address contemporary forms of racism and racial discrimination, including algorithmic bias and, finally, the right to justice and material, moral, and spiritual reparation for harm derived from trans-Atlantic trafficking, enslavement, and the prolongation of its consequences. In that sense, the Declaration is projected as the cornerstone of the third generation of rights of Afro-descendants, which will be focused on restorative justice, an issue that promises to be the gravitational axis of the human rights agenda in the coming decades.

The path towards the declaration also has the potential to contribute to the reconstruction of the bridge between Africans and people of African descent, and to the consensus and adoption of a common agenda around key issues such as reparations, which transcends the people of African descent themselves. It is a rare opportunity to engage in frank and constructive dialogue with states and other interested parties.

The content of the draft declaration seeks to protect all people who identify themselves as Afro-descendants. In its preamble, it alludes to the legal, contextual, situational, institutional, and instrumental framework that constitutes the current architecture of the rights of Afro-descendants in the global system for the protection of human rights.[89] It also reaffirms the validity of the universal principles of human rights;[90] condemns systemic or structural racism;[91] and outlines the aspirational goals of people of African descent.[92]

The Draft Declaration covers the wide range of political, economic, social, cultural, and environmental rights of people of African descent, as well as the right to equitable participation in the benefits derived from access to traditional knowledge associated with genetic resources.[93] It also seeks to encompass climate justice and contemporary forms of racism and racial discrimination, particularly algorithmic bias.

Contentious issues in the formulation of the declaration are related to the position of several delegations, particularly the Western Group, which resist the recognition of Afro-descendants as a collective subject. They insist on ascribing them to the

---

[88] General Recommendation 34 on racism and racial discrimination against people of African descent. Accessed 07 July 2025. Available from: https://www.refworld.org/es/leg/coment/cerd/2011/es/83463.

[89] See Elements for the draft United Nations declaration on the respect, protection and fulfillment of the human rights of people of African descent Annex I to the "Status report of the Intergovernmental Working Group on the Effective Implementation of the Durban Declaration and Programme of Action on the elaboration of the draft United Nations declaration on the respect, protection, and fulfilment of the human rights of people of African descent", A/79/304, 09 August 2024. https://docs.un.org/en/A/79/304. Accessed 07 July 2025.

[90] Ibid.

[91] Ibid.

[92] Ibid.

[93] Ibid.

mere condition of individuals. Consistent with this position, they refuse to allow the Declaration to incorporate the concepts of 'peoples' and free self-determination. The same bloc opposes the recognition of collective rights, in clear contrast to the principles of diversity and legal pluralism. Indeed, in South America, the rights stated here enjoy constitutional and legal roots in many countries.

Likewise, as expected, the Western Group opposes the declaration's recognition of the right to reparation for damages of the trans-Atlantic trafficking and enslavement of persons of African heritage. It is also surprising that despite the state of the global conversation on climate change and the critical importance that the ancestral territories of people of African descent have for the sustainability of the planet, several delegations from the same Western Group oppose the provisions related to climate justice. Some delegations, particularly from countries with theocratic governments, veto any reference to gender and intersectionality. There is also a reduced assessment of the scope of systemic racism experienced by Afro-descendants.

Gaps identified in the Draft Declaration include (1) lack of a definition of Afro-descendants. (2) underdevelopment of the issue of artificial intelligence and algorithmic bias; (3) in depth analysis of the subject of traumas of enslavement, which lacks indicators for its evaluation and monitoring.

In this regard, it is worth highlighting some preliminary observations of the Permanent Forum on People of African Descent on the Declaration:

- First, the Forum echoes the voices that the Declaration must pay tribute to the origins of the discourse of persons of African descent, recognize the importance of the Durban Declaration and Programme of Action, and highlight the historical injustices of slavery, colonization, and dispossession.[94]
- Second, it maintains that the full and effective implementation of the International Convention on the Elimination of All Forms of Racial Discrimination and the Durban Declaration and Programme of Action remain essential to addressing racial discrimination against people of African descent. It is necessary to comprehensively recognize, monitor and effectively combat systemic and structural racial discrimination at the local, national, regional, and global levels.[95]
- Third, it attaches great importance to the preparation of a declaration that complements, expands, and completes the current human rights instruments relating to people of African descent. The declaration should also mention the notions of identity, recognition, equality, and non-discrimination; the right to life and security, including physical and mental health, and intergenerational trauma; the right to culture and history; the rights to participation and self-determination; the right to equality in the distribution of economic goods and progress; and the right to justice.[96]
- Fourth, the Forum reaffirms the need to (1) recognize the collective and individual rights of people of African descent, (2) effectively combat systemic and

[94] Report of the Permanent Forum on People of African Descent on its first and second sessions, A/HRC/54/68, 16 August 2023, para. 24. Available from: https://docs.un.org/en/A/HRC/54/68.

[95] Ibid para. 51.

[96] Ibid para. 24.

structural racial discrimination against people of African descent; (3) protect, in certain social contexts, collective cultural, religious, territorial, and environmental rights, among others, and (4) empower people of African descent in the development, application and monitoring of policies that concern them.[97]
- Fifth, the Forum affirms that reparation is a cornerstone of justice in the twenty-first century and that, without it, the sustainable development agenda cannot be effective. As recognized in the Durban Declaration and Programme of Action, comprehensive restorative justice is necessary to achieve the full realization of the dignity and human rights of people of African descent. The Forum affirms that slavery, the trans-Atlantic trade in enslaved Africans, apartheid, and colonialism were crimes against humanity and constituted genocide.[98]
- Sixth, in the opinion of the Permanent Forum, the Declaration should reflect other issues related to people of African descent, in particular, their recognition as peoples and their right to self-determination; digital inclusion, modern forms of racism and racial discrimination, including algorithmic bias, predictive policing and, more generally, the inappropriate use of artificial intelligence tools; and the right to obtain reparation for the consequences of colonialism, the Trans-Atlantic slave trade and the enslavement of people of African descent.[99]

The United Nations Declaration on the Promotion, Protection, and Full Respect of the Human Rights of People of African Descent therefore represents an exceptional opportunity towards a third generation of rights based on restorative justice.

8 Conclusion

The Third World Conference against Racism, Racial Discrimination, and other related forms of Intolerance and its preparatory conferences, in particular, the Regional Conference, held in Santiago, Chile in 2000, represented a qualitative leap in the process of consolidating a globalizing vision of the validity of the challenges presented by racism and racial discrimination.

During the Durban process, the African diaspora, around 300 million people, who until then remained in the shadows, today enjoy recognition as an individual and collective subject of international law. Legal and institutional frameworks have been adopted for their benefit at the national and regional levels, and instrumental progress is being made at the international level. Along this path, the role of the Social Movement of Afro-descendants that emerged in the preparatory conferences and in the Durban Conference itself has been decisive. Future impacts would be directly proportional to the collective action of Afro-descendants and their ability to reach a consensus on an agenda, which today is stated around the demands for

[97] Ibid para 51.

[98] Ibid para 50.

[99] Note 85 above para. 24.

restorative justice and the creativity that the said movement can deploy, to weave alliances with various social sectors and politicians.

Durban recognized that people of African descent were victims of colonialism and enslavement and continue to be victims of its consequences. Today, particularly after the global mobilization after the murder of George Floyd in the United States, there is a growth in collective global anti-racist consciousness. Parallel to this, today we are witnessing an escalation of conflicts, where the denial of the human essence is once again at the center of geopolitics and seriously threatens international peace and security.

Tensions converge with new global challenges including large-scale migration; the climate crisis; the political instrumentalization of racism, which includes the theory of demographic reconversion or replacement; the loss of confidence in democracy and institutions; tensions around gender and ethnic identities; the aging of the population in some regions of the world; and the disruptive impacts of artificial intelligence, in particular, concerning inequality and algorithmic bias, which results in contemporary forms of discrimination.

For multiple reasons, Africans and people of African descent, who together represent the largest population group globally, that is, around 1.6 billion people, find themselves at the center of such challenges.[100] It should be noted that Africans and Afro-descendants are located in key areas for the energy transition, due to their wealth in natural resources. Many Afro-descendant communities are located in geographical areas of special importance for the supply chain, due to their intersection with several of the main ports such as the Panama Canal, particularly in South America. Africans and Afro-descendants have a demographic bonus due to having the youngest population.

The advancement of a second international decade of people of African descent and the process towards a "United Nations Declaration on the Promotion, Protection and Full Respect of the Human Rights of People of African Descent", hopefully of the "peoples", are of the greatest importance on the path towards deepening recognition, justice and development of people of African descent and are an exceptional opportunity to deepen the impacts of Durban. In this regard, it is worth highlighting the following developments, with a view to collective action:

1. **Update of the Programme of Activities for the Second International Decade for People of African Descent.** Under the responsibility of the Office of the High Commissioner for Human Rights and the presidency of the General Assembly, in accordance with Resolution 79/193,[101] which proclaimed the Second Decade.
2. **Formulation of a United Nations Declaration on the Promotion, Protection and Full Respect of the Human Rights of People of African Descent.** This is envisioned as the universal framework that will compile the standards on the

[100] See UN PFPAD Expert Consultation Proceedings and Written Submissions, p. 133. Accessed 10 June 2025. Available from: https://hrp.law.harvard.edu/wp-content/uploads/2024/10/UN-PFPAD-Expert-Consultation-Proceedings-and-Written-Submissions_digitally-accessible_.pdf.

[101] https://docs.un.org/en/A/RES/79/193.

rights of people of African descent. It is currently under development by the Intergovernmental Working Group on the Follow-up to the Durban Declaration, United Nations. It originated in document A/67/18, CERD 2012.[102]

3. **Formulation of the Inter-American Declaration on People of African Descent.** Resolution AG/RES 3028 (LIV-O/24)[103] of the General Assembly of the Organization of American States (OAS) calls on Member States to establish an informal Working Group, with the support of the Department of Social Inclusion (DIS) of the OAS and in consultation with civil society and other social actors, with the purpose of drafting an Inter-American Declaration on People of African Descent. This process is expected to incorporate the perspectives and visions of the States in order to promote and protect the human rights of Afro-descendant individuals and communities throughout the region, adopting an intersectional approach and recognizing the specific situations of vulnerability faced by Afro-descendant populations. The ultimate objective is to address the persistent and structural causes of systemic racism and related inequalities in the region. In line with this mandate, and under the leadership of Colombia and Brazil, the OAS Permanent Council has carried out consultations with Member States and civil society with a view to gathering their inputs on the content of the Declaration and is currently moving forward with the development of a roadmap for this purpose.
4. **Influence on the legal, institutional, instrumental architecture and governance related to reparatory justice; climate and environmental justice; and artificial intelligence (AI).** In this regard, there is support for the creation of a Multi-Donor Fund for Haiti.
5. **Implementation of decision** CBD/COP/16/L.7,[104] which recognizes the role of people of African descent, comprising [collectives] embodying traditional lifestyles in the implementation of the Convention on Biological Diversity, its "implementation in some countries, with positive contributions at the global level, as well as in the implementation of national biodiversity strategies and action plans", and "their shared knowledge and connection with their lands in the implementation of the Convention on Biological Diversity and the Kunming-Montreal Global Biodiversity Framework".[105]
6. Formulation of an Encyclical on the role of the Catholic Church in trafficking and enslavement. CERD/C/VAT/CO/16-23[106] is currently in progress.

[102] https://www.refworld.org/reference/annualreport/cerd/2012/en/89514.

[103] https://www.refworld.org/sites/default/files/2024-12/14806.pdf.

[104] https://www.cbd.int/doc/c/a62f/bee7/68313dec1e3b0689049feba1/cop-16-l-07-en.pdf.

[105] CBD/COP/16/L.7.

[106] https://docs.un.org/en/CERD/C/VAT/CO/16-23.

References

Bello A (2005) Santiago+5 pre-conference framework document against racism, the xenophobia, discrimination and intolerance. Pre-Joint Secretariat Santiago + 5 conference against racism, xenophobia, discrimination and intolerance. https://poblacionafroperuana.cultura.pe/sites/default/files/santiago_5_0.pdf

De La Fuente A (2018) The rise of Afro-Latin America *ReVista*. 12-13-17_spreads_low_res.pdf. Accessed 28 June 2025

El País (2025, November 1) La sangrienta emboscada de la policía de Río en la Sierra de la Misericordia. https://elpais.com/america/2025-11-01/la-sangrienta-emboscada-de-la-policia-derio-en-la-sierra-de-la-misericordia.html

Fórum Brasileiro de Segurança Pública (2025) Anuário Brasileiro de Segurança Pública 2025. Fórum Brasileiro de Segurança Pública

Freire G, Schwartz Orellana S, Carbonari F (2022) Afro-descendant inclusion in education: an anti-racist agenda for Latin America, 31 December 2022. https://documents1.worldbank.org/curated/en/099056005022316092/pdf/IDU05497146208ea8042190919d0d27079d7a405.pdf. Accessed 27 June 2025

Organization of American States [OAS]; and Inter-American Commission on Human Rights [IACHR] (2011) The situation of people of African descent in the Americas. OAS/Ser.L/V/II. Doc. 62. https://www.oas.org/es/cidh/afrodescendientes/docs/pdf/afros_2011_esp.pdf

Ramos, et al. (2025) Pele Alvo: crônicas de dor e luta. Rede de Observatórios da Segurança

Making the Most of the Legendary Leadership and Legacy of Durban: What Next?

Barbara G. Reynolds

> *"I am no longer accepting the things I cannot change. I am changing the things I cannot accept."—Angela Davis*

The memories of the legends of Durban—the 2001 Conference Against Racism, Racial Discrimination, Xenophobia and Related Intolerance held in Durban South Africa from August 31 to September 7—speak for themselves.

On December 6, 2024 at the Memoirs of Durban, the now traditional commemoration of the Durban Conference held during the annual public session of the United Nations Working Group of experts on people of African descent, participants of the Durban Conference spoke of the euphoria, excitement, energy and enthusiasm that engulfed them as they headed to Durban. The session benefited from the testimonies of six participants who were present in Durban in 2001. These participants shared the passion and dynamism of the Durban Conference in 2001. They related the attempts to shift them from their stated intent and purpose, and how they were able to respond and move onto other priorities.

In his remarks as Convenor of the 2024 Durban Memoirs, HE Ambassador Brian Wallace, Permanent Representative of Jamaica to the United Nations focused on the imperative of clarity and unity of purpose in the pursuit of reparatory justice. He mentioned two essential streams, namely, the first that honours the Durban Declaration and Programme of Action (DDPA), the principal output of the Durban Conference, as an institution and a foundation; and the second is the imperative to unpack the DDPA to transform its substantive content into actions that will deliver the DDPA outcomes. To achieve this, HE Ambassador Wallace reminded participants of the need to be strategic, and to work in tandem with diplomats negotiating in the international space, particularly at the United Nations, ensuring that the basic tenets of divide and conquer that buttressed slavery and colonisation do not continue

B. G. Reynolds (✉)
United Nations Working Group of Experts on People of African Descent, Geneva, Switzerland

C. S. Namakula (ed.), *Untold Reflections from the World Conference Against Racism*, SpringerBriefs in Law, https://doi.org/10.1007/978-3-032-17265-5_8

to divide people of African descent. HE Ambassador Wallace pledged his support, specifying the following areas that Jamaica was keen to support, namely, efforts to quantify the damages, by region, by country; engagement with the perpetrating countries; maintaining a repository of partners, institutional or individual, who can help to solidify a global coalition; and, engaging with those countries and institutions that have secured some success and the lessons learned from their experiences.

While not legally binding, the Durban Declaration is a clear statement about the prevalence of all forms of racism across the globe and the moral imperative for counter measures to fight racism and its impact on all sectors of society and all aspects of daily life worldwide. The Durban Declaration was not the first global statement on racism—after all the Universal Declaration on Human Rights (1948), the two International Covenants on political, civil, economic, cultural and social rights (1966, 1976), the International Convention on the Elimination of All Forms of Racial Discrimination (1965), and the people-specific conventions which focused on women (CEDAW, 1979), children (CRC, 1989), persons with disabilities (CRPD, 2006) and indigenous persons (UNDRIP, 2007) all eschew discrimination on the basis of race. Similarly, there were two world conferences against racism, organized by UNESCO in 1978 and 1983, and two since Durban, organized by the UN in 2009 and 2021.[1] Further, the World Conference on Human Rights (Vienna, 1993) and its Declaration and Programme of Action called attention to racism. Amidst all of these global moments, Durban stands out.

So, then what was so special about the Durban Conference and the DDPA? First, beyond the substance, the symbolism of holding a world conference against racism in Durban, South Africa where one of the most peculiar and egregious forms of racism—apartheid—had been meted out to and largely reversed by Black Africans was momentous. The Durban Conference attracted a concerted participation of Africans and people of African descent from across the globe. They had planned, caucused, mobilized, strategized and turned out in significant numbers to speak out and speak up with a noticeable degree of coherence and consistence on the issues that were most important to Black people across the globe.

The Durban Conference and the DDPA were the first instance when the issue of reparations for enslavement and colonization was explicitly addressed on the world stage. In this regard, the Durban Declaration made three significant contributions to efforts to provide redress for enslavement, colonization and racial segregation. First, it acknowledged that slavery and the slave trade, especially the trans-Atlantic slave trade are a crime against humanity because of their barbaric nature, their magnitude, their organized nature and violation of the very humanity of those who suffered this egregious harm.[2] Second, the Declaration indicated the imperative of providing just and adequate reparation for the slave trade.[3] Third, and very importantly, the

---

[1] Durban Review Conference, 20–24 April 2009. https://www.un.org/en/durbanreview2009/. Accessed 11 June 2025. Global Forum against Racism and Discrimination | UNESCO. https://www.unesco.org/en/forum-against-racism-discrimination. Accessed 11 June 2025.

[2] Paragraph 1, Durban Declaration and Programme of Action (DDPA).

[3] Paragraph 104, ibid.

preamble explicitly acknowledged “that no derogation from the prohibition of racial discrimination, genocide, the crime of apartheid and slavery is permitted, as defined in the obligations under the relevant human rights instruments”.

For people of African descent and for Africans, the Durban Conference and the proclamation of the DDPA was a watershed moment. In spite of claims to the contrary and efforts to undermine the DDPA, or worse, to nullify its validity and utility as a global human rights instrument, the Durban Conference and the DDPA are to be commemorated, celebrated and used for the purposes for which they were intended, including honouring the global consensus, and those who were present, who stood up and continue to stand up to defend the integrity of the Conference and the outcome.

The legacy of the Durban Conference for Africans and people of African descent is an enduring one. There is greater awareness of their concerns and claims among people outside of the UN system, particularly human rights activists, advocates, educators and scholars. Civil society organisations around the globe continue to discharge their commitments to ensure greater public awareness, and greater response among governments. While this has been, inevitably, a patchwork quilt of ideas and agendas, the efforts are coalescing, largely because of the mechanisms established by the UN Commission on Human Rights/UN Human Rights Council. In particular, the Working Group of experts on people of African descent has produced a prodigious body of work—at time of writing, comprising some 25 country visits, over 100 communications urging Member States and others to investigate and take necessary action to protect the human rights of people of African descent, 23 ground-breaking thematic reports and a number of data sets—all of which continue to provide a basis for education and advocacy for people of African descent.[4] One of the priorities of the Working Group in its early years was its tremendous advocacy, alongside civil society organisations, for a permanent forum and for an international decade on people of African descent. The materialization of the permanent forum has in turn provided new opportunities for greater advocacy for people of African descent.

The (now first) international decade on people of African descent, 2015–2024, focused on three priorities—recognition, justice and development, and the renewal of the decade for 2025–2034 reflects a similar commitment.[5] Considerable progress has been made in several areas. However, these achievements fall far behind what was anticipated as people of African descent worldwide continue to face structural and systemic racialized barriers in the pursuit of their human rights. In many areas where considerable progress has been made, there are growing efforts to remove or reverse positive measures intended to level ground for people of African descent. This is evident in the dismantling of long-accepted legal provisions, the erosion of investment in diversity, equality and inclusion principles and programmes, and the

[4] See Report of the Working Group of experts on people of African descent: 20 years of facilitating the journey from rhetoric to reality in the fight against racism, A/HRC/54/71, 17 August 2023.

[5] Proclamation of the Second International Decade for People of African Descent, A/RES/79/193, 23 December 2024.

spurious recrafting of the history of people of African descent. For example, in the US, there are reports of legal challenges, using civil rights provisions to claim anti-white discrimination and to pervert the use as a basis for inclusion of disadvantaged groups. Very surprisingly, there continues to be concerted effort, with limited effect, to disenfranchise people of African descent. Explicit teaching about race, racism, African studies, and related content are being leached out of curricular.

Knowledge of the first decade was not widespread at international, national, and local levels. Even in countries with significant Afro-descendent populations, awareness of the Decade was sparse and spotty, with very little perceptible effort by member states to publicly embrace the opportunity to promote the rights of people of African descent. Thus, the very object and purpose of the Decade were largely defeated, and there are few policies, programmes and structures that were established specifically for its promotion and implementation. Activities directly or indirectly related to the Decade have not been systematically documented.

Finally, the inadequate quantity and quality of data on people of African descent is a major constraint. While some countries do not disaggregate data by race/ethnicity, in other instances, particularly in less affluent countries, data on race, race relations, and the impact of face on access to goods and services, among several other critical ways, are just not collected and analysed. These data are lacking in the most basic areas, because they are not systematically collected and analysed.

Recognition is the foundational pillar of the Decade, and encompasses voice, visibility, views and votes. For most people groups, recognition is grounded in constitutions, legislation and legal and policy frameworks at all levels of the government and across all spheres of public life. While most constitutions protect race and/or ethnicity, skin colour and hair texture are generally not protected, and are often the trigger for Afrophobia and racial discrimination. The anticipated outcome of the recognition pillar was the visibility and the active voice of people of African descent across all aspects of political, civic, economic, social and cultural life at community and national levels. Beginning with accurate reflection in census and other population data sets, recognition meant inclusion in voter registration.

Recognition encompasses the respectful and accurate representation of the history and culture of people of African descent, their role in societal development and their contribution to all aspects of being, knowing, doing and living together. In this regard, inclusion of people of African descent and their cultures in the curricular of primary and secondary schools, the introduction or maintenance and revitalization of African studies programmes at university level, and the research by people of African descent on their own issues are still largely unsupported and unfunded. As the Working Group highlights in its Operational Guidelines for the inclusion of people of African Descent in the 2030 Agenda, "Education has a critical role in mental liberation and symbolic decolonization".[6]

[6] See Operational Guidelines on inclusion of People of African Descent in the 2030 agenda, Working Group of experts on people of African descent, adopted on 09 December 2020, p. 23. https://www.ohchr.org/sites/default/files/Documents/Issues/Racism/WGEAPD/Guidelines_inclusion_2030_Agenda.pdf. Accessed 11 June 2025.

Recognition through legislative and legal instruments triggers the need for up-to-date, relevant policies, programmes, procedures and processes and the concomitant budgetary provision, high-level attention and diverse expertise. To achieve this fully, collection of data disaggregated by race, is required, and censuses ought to include modules that elicit accurate and relevant information about the presence of people of African heritage. Adequate budgetary provisions, and eventually funding are essential to the provision of accessible and affordable basic goods and services. In all these areas, the recognition of people of African descent lags behind most other groups, including in instances where they are a visible minority or numerical majority.

Many people of African descent are invisible or have been erased, their voices unheard, silent, or silenced. On the other hand, people of African descent are rendered hyper-visible in negative contexts, such as criminal behaviour and or impoverished social settings. While they excel in the arts, sports, science, technology and public service, participation is not commensurate with the gravity of their concerns, the size of their populations or their expertise and talents. In government, justice, industry, commerce, trade, and economic development, even in instances where they are a numerical majority, people of African descent are further behind because of under-representation, institutionalized racism, Afrophobia and anti-black discrimination. The issue of the representation of people of African descent, both how they are represented in decision-making processes as well as how they are portrayed, often feeds into and off of their invisibility and absence of their voice.

Although the national legislation of most UN member states generally recognizes the human rights of all citizens, this is not translated into policies and programmes that promote the rights of people of African descent. There is widespread denial of justice on a range of issues, with men of African descent disproportionately subjected to police brutality, arrest, compromised legal proceedings and incarceration. Economic, social, and cultural justice lags much further behind, with few violations in these spheres making it to the courts because legal protections are inadequate, human rights and legal literacy is limited, unconscious and conscious bias is widespread, and the cost of legal representation is prohibitive.

The development envisaged in the Durban Declaration and Programme of Action is anchored in the 1986 Declaration on the Right to Development and it envisions the active, free and meaningful participation of people of African descent, like any other group, in decision-making about their political, social, economic and cultural life,[7] and in the fair distribution of resultant benefits.[8] The DDPA explicitly identified poverty as both cause and consequence of discrimination;[9] while emphasizing the need to address education, employment, health and housing as essential

[7] Paragraph 34, DDPA.

[8] Programme of Activities for the Implementation of the International Decade for People of African Descent, A/RES/69/16, 01 December 2014, para 19.

[9] Ibid para 18.

elements of development that are impacted by racism, racial discrimination, xenophobia and related intolerance.[10]

Despite achievements in education, people of African descent are disproportionately behind on health and nutrition, employment and income, access to credit, ownership of material assets and wealth creation. In sports and the arts, where people of African descent excel and in the uniformed services where their patriotism shines, they still face rank racism and discrimination. In governance, they remain largely invisible, their voice, views and vote largely discounted. There is considerable debate about the relevance and adequacy of education, which in turn affects employability and employment. Further, there is evidence, of the worsening situation of people of African descent when race intersects with gender, religious or political affiliation, age, migrant status, and sexual orientation, particularly in economic development.

Access to decent, affordable housing is a major challenge for people of African descent across the globe. In developed countries, this is mainly due to legal and illegal redistricting, gentrification of traditional black neighbourhoods and the cost of borrowing. In addition to the inadequacy of housing, the adequacy and affordability of the most basic goods and services *de facto* segregate people of African descent from other racial groups in many parts of the world. Forced to live in *ghettos*, shanty-towns, high density areas, favelas, slums and sub-human public housing, not only do people of African descent face social discrimination, but the cumulative and multiplier effect on every other aspect of twenty-first century life undermines their agency in their own development.

The failures of the International Decade on People of African Descent (2015–2024), in general terms, hinged on three factors: (1) the failure of Member States to recognise, promulgate, promote and support the Decade; (2) the reluctance of many to conceptualise the implementation of the Decade as a matter of human rights of people of African descent and therefore as an obligation on the part of states and not charity or goodwill; and, (3) the constant chipping away at the DDPA, the undermining of Durban mechanisms, and consequently the Decade itself, a reality that arguably verges on the erasure of advancements of the collective cause of people of African descent at the highest level.

It is against this background that the UN General Assembly declared a second decade for people of African descent (2025–2034).[11] To be effective, a second decade must have at least five essential dimensions:

- First, the priorities and the programme of action of the decade must be negotiated with the input of people of African descent, through adequate consultation and with the support of the designated human rights mechanisms. This second decade must be promulgated by Member States at national and sub-national levels, translated where necessary into national languages and non-technical versions.
- Second, Member States must invest politically, financially, and technically, in the activities of the decade, intentionally rehabilitating state and civil institutions,

[10] Ibid para 31.

[11] A/RES/79/193, 23 December 2024.

spaces and places, legislation, policies and programmes, perspectives and attitudes, and particularly in the development of people of African descent. Third, governments must guarantee and assure the respect and protection of the rights of activists and advocates for people of African descent. Fourth, the adoption of the Declaration on the Promotion, Protection and Full Respect of the Human Rights of People of African Descent.

The declaration of a second decade for people of African descent is already wrought with challenges. It is significant that (a) South Africa, a frontline advocate since Durban, was not one of the sponsors of the resolution, (b) there was no prior consultation with civil society about the priorities, (c) the continuation of the focus of the first decade is a compromise.

A second decade must find its grounding in the adoption of a UN declaration on the rights of people of African descent. The declaration should espouse the right to development,[12] and the right to a clean, healthy and sustainable environment.[13] It should also envelop at least four pillars: (1) racial justice that addresses the unfinished agenda of this first decade, (2) reparatory justice that explicitly rights historical wrongs, (3) environmental justice that puts arrests and hopefully reverses environmental degradation in order to leave a livable world for generations to come, (4) digital (in)justice that addresses the new and emerging technologies that can enhance or undermine every positive development the human race has achieved thus far, and (5) spatial (in)justice that addresses bias in organization and utilization of physical space by various social groups and identities.

The success of the second decade will depend on adequate collection, analysis and dissemination of data on race, racism and discrimination, and examining trends, outcomes and impact, including trans-generational impact. There is also the need for funding, in developing and developed countries, for research by people of African descent about the issues affecting their wellbeing and development.

To achieve this, governments and state institutions, international organisations, the corporate and civil sectors must integrate race/ethnicity/colour as a demographic marker into analytical and planning frameworks, funding and resourcing decisions, and the conceptualisation, implementation, monitoring and evaluation of programmes at institutional, community, and societal levels. This requires immediate and short-term interventions and positioning, with medium term to long-term investment in public education, policy and legislative reform, in training and retraining people, in monitoring and evaluation, and in recognising, affirming and rewarding progress. This begins with a simple first step, namely the acceptance of the inherent agency of people of African descent in their own development and an appreciation of their contribution to our collective human development.

Another major area of focus, as in the DDPA regarding indigenous peoples,[14] is the proposed declaration on the promotion and full respect of the human rights of

[12] A/RES/41/128 (04 December 1986), A/RES/71/192 (19 January 2017).

[13] A/HRC/RES/48/13 (18 October 2021).

[14] See para 206, Durban Declaration and Programme of Action, 2001.

people of African descent. The importance of a declaration on the rights of people of African descent cannot be overestimated for two reasons. First, despite the allusion to race in existing conventions, the non-realization of human rights by people of African descent because of structural, systemic and systematic racism. Secondly, the specificities and peculiarities in which anti-Black, anti-African racism and discrimination (Afrophobia) manifest themselves must be articulated if specific measures are to be taken to eliminate these and reverse their negative effect.

Led by the Intergovernmental Working Group on the Effective Implementation of the Durban Declaration and Programme of Action, progress on the drafting has been steady, initially steered by Rwanda and at the time of writing by Kenya. The challenges in this process emanate largely from the 'great powers', which curiously object to the inclusion of the right to development or the right to a clean and healthy environment, or to the idea of 'collective' rights. It is expected that these objections will dissipate, as well as the bottlenecks being encountered around the use of the term 'intersectionality'.

One of the most important emerging trends in the early 2020s is the increasing leadership that African Member States are playing in addressing the legacy of trans-Atlantic slavery, colonization and racial segregation. The distinctions between Africans, diaspora Africans and people of African descent are at best trifling and superficial and at worst spurious, pejorative and divisive. Whatever the calculus and compromise that was necessary to remove Africans from the follow-up of the Durban Conference, the history and therefore the future of Africans, diaspora Africans and people of African descent are inextricably linked, and these distinctions have run their course. The Africa Union's Sixth Region is not mere fanfare but an essential part of Africa, and policies and programmes emanating from the Africa Union augur well for the future.[15]

So, what next? There are a few caveats well worth repeating over and over. First, people of African descent are not monochromatic or monolithic. There is much diversity among Black people, on issues that vary from skin colour or hair texture (and their lingering clout) to religion, political views, socio-economic status, and a myriad other things. Yet, both people of African descent and others continue to be surprised, even indignant, when this diversity shows up.

Second, not all skin folk are kin folk. There is a growing number of Black people ready to trumpet the agenda of those whose actions are inimical to the collective wellbeing of Black/people. Some of these are influential positions, others are paid influencers, some having climbed the ladder of affirmative action or other initiatives, are ready to kick it to the curb once they reach their pinnacle of success. It is not that there has not always been those who betray the cause. The problem today is the rate at which their disinformation and misinformation spins out of control, trapping many in their toxic webs.

Third, the schisms within are detracting and distracting. There is considerable competition among those who purport to support the cause, providing they are the visible face. These are the individuals who have set themselves up as the interlocutors or spokespersons of people of African descent. This is a growing challenge of

[15] See Namakula (2024), pp. 424–446. Available from: https://www.ahrlj.up.ac.za/namakula-cs.

some complexity and calls for explicit and coordinated effort for healing within the Black community. Fourth, advocacy for people of African descent benefits all people. Fifth, people of African descent welcome others who support their cause, as much as people of African descent stand in solidarity with others.

Moving forward, there are four priorities that stand out:

- First, there must be a good faith effort at the level of the UN to pursue reparatory justice to right historical wrongs.
- Second, as the review of the decade shows, racism, Afrophobia and discrimination persist. Thus, pursuing racial justice remains a priority.
- Third, many people of African descent live in areas that are acutely affected by climate change. Others live in areas affected by excessive legal and illegal extractive industries. Pursuing environmental and spatial justice is a priority.
- Fourth, and finally, the pursuit of digital justice is emerging as a major priority.

The shared history requires that we define our shared principles. Our inherent diversity requires that we follow pathways that will converge and diverge, intersect and parallel one another. Undergirding these four collective priorities, it is essential that education for employability and employment, economic development ground all thinking and initiatives. Without education, without viable employment (including self-employment), without economic viability, gains are easily erased. The road ahead is not that difficult. We have come a long way! We can stay the course!

Reports

Operational Guidelines on inclusion of People of African Descent in the 2030 agenda, Working Group of experts on people of African descent, adopted on 09 December 2020. https://www.ohchr.org/sites/default/files/Documents/Issues/Racism/WGEAPD/Guidelines_inclusion_2030_Agenda.pdf. Accessed 11 June 2025.

Proclamation of the Second International Decade for People of African Descent, A/RES/79/193, 23 December 2024.

Programme of Activities for the Implementation of the International Decade for People of African Descent, A/RES/69/16, 01 December 2014.

Report of the Working Group of experts on people of African descent: 20 years of facilitating the journey from rhetoric to reality in the fight against racism, A/HRC/54/71, 17 August 2023.

Reference

Namakula CS (2024) Expounding the frontiers of the human rights agenda of the African Union for the extra-Africa diaspora. Afr Hum Rights Law J 24:424–446

MIX
Papier aus verantwortungsvollen Quellen
Paper from responsible sources
FSC® C105338

If you have any concerns about our products,
you can contact us on
ProductSafety@springernature.com

In case Publisher is established outside the EU,
the EU authorized representative is:
Springer Nature Customer Service Center GmbH
Europaplatz 3, 69115 Heidelberg, Germany

Printed by Libri Plureos GmbH
in Hamburg, Germany